THE HOLLYWOOD EYE

What Makes Movies Work

JON BOORSTIN

 Cornelia & Michael Bessie Books

An Imprint of HarperCollins*Publishers*

Photo credits follow the index.

FIRST EDITION

DESIGNED BY JOEL AVIROM

Illustrations by Roger Allers

Library of Congress Cataloging-in-Publication Data

Boorstin, Jon, 1946-
The Hollywood eye: what makes movies work/Jon Boorstin.—1st ed.
p.   cm.
"A Cornelia & Michael Bessie book."
ISBN 0-06-039113-8
1. Motion pictures—Production and direction.   2. Motion pictures—
Philosophy.   3. Cinematography.   I. Title.
PN1995.9.P7B63   1990
791.43—dc20   89-46075

90 91 92 93 94 DT/MPC 10 9 8 7 6 5 4 3 2 1

To
Leni

CONTENTS

ACKNOWLEDGMENTS

*A*ngry writers have often depicted Hollywood as a cruel and inhospitable place; the wildly successful, Oscar-laden recipients of its bounty have described it as a sort of love feast, a no-business-like-show-business town filled with the most wonderful people in the world. For most of us, of course, it's neither. It's a working environment with its own peculiar rewards and frustrations. But one of the things that drew me to Hollywood as a young man and which continues to appeal to me is that traditionally in Hollywood you learn by doing. Film schools have changed the balance some, but it's still a town where you are supposed to learn by apprenticing yourself to experienced folk rather than by reading and passing exams. It's almost medieval in that regard. And moviemaking is complicated and absorbing enough that people in the industry are eager to pool their knowledge.

Consequently, the acknowledgments listed here aren't only a way of expressing my gratitude to those who helped me, they're a record of the principal sources for this book. That's not to say that those I thank agree with everything I've written. But what I know that I haven't learned by trial and error, these people have taught me. They are my bibliography, as it were.

First, I'd like to thank those who have taken the time and trouble to read the book in manuscript and give me their comments: Tom Baum, Michael Bessie, Ron Blumer, Anna Boorstin, Daniel Boorstin, Paul Boorstin, Ruth Boorstin, Howard Chesley, Pieter Jan Brugge, Dr. Evan Cameron, Surendar Chawdhary, Andrew Z. Davis, Dennis Feldman, Amy Gash, Betty Goldberg, Greg Mac-

Gillivray, Muffy Meyer, Jeanine Oppewal, Richard Pearce, Phil Alden Robinson, Eric Saarinen, Peter Schneider, Dr. James Scott, Ellen Shapiro, Hope Tschopik.

Michael Chapman, Fred Fuchs, Alexander Mackendrick, and Ken Zunder also gave me information essential to the writing of this book. Diana Leszczynski was tenacious and resourceful in searching out the photos. Roger Allers, with patience, skills, and understanding honed as a storyboard artist, created the illustrations.

You learn something, bad or good, from everyone you work with. But over the years there have been some who have gone out of their way to explain their craft to me, whether it was recording sound, cutting a scene, or shaping a script or a deal. In addition to those friends who helped me with the manuscript, I'd like to thank Angelo Corrao, Lou Lombardo, Trudy Ship, Jack Wheeler, Bob Wolfe, Karen Wookey for initiating me into the mysteries of editing film; Sean Daniel, Gordon Davidson, Jack Garfein, Amy Jones, Robert Redford, and Holly Sloan the mysteries of story and character; George Jenkins the mysteries of production design; Michael Small the mysteries of movie music, and George Brand, Les Fresholtz, Bud Grenzbach, Tom Overton the mysteries of movie sound; Fred Bernstein, Tom Hansen, Michael Simpson, David Wardlow, Eric Weisman the mysteries of movie chemistry and the deal.

Above all, a special thanks to David Freeman for his patient support and insightful advice; to Eric Saarinen and Gordon Willis for their hours spent divulging the secrets of shooting film; and to Charles Eames, Terry Sanders, and Alan Pakula, who let me learn by doing at considerable risk to their own good names and peace of mind.

INTRODUCTION

MAKING MOVIES WORK

I think I remember the happiest moment of my childhood. I was sitting in a dark movie theater between my father and mother, eating an ice-cream cone. I looked up at my parents, edged with the glow from the screen; I licked the sweet wetness; I felt the sounds from the screen wash over me, and I was overcome by the awesome rightness of things. Engulfed by that dark space I indulged in glorious private pleasures, yet I was not alone. I was protected, but I was free. I felt my soul expand to fill the room.

I don't remember the movie. I'm not sure the movie even mattered. What mattered was the thrill of that special transaction with the screen. What did I give up? What did I get in return? I've spent most of my adult life asking myself those questions, one way or another. But the more time I spend making movies the farther I get from answers. That glow is gone with childhood, and the more I devote myself to the craft of movies the harder it is to recapture those naive emotions.

But I know, as my fellow film workers know, that distant thrill isn't just why we're at the work, it is why our audience goes to the movies. In order to do our jobs we fight to hold on to what is left of that original feeling at any cost. Some turn to drugs to conjure it up, some become aggressively infantile to coddle it along, but most of us with a job to do can't afford such self-indulgence. Instead, the minutiae of filmmaking become the battleground for the struggle. We find echoes of the old pleasure in the new pleasures of creation and dissection. The question becomes not "Is it wonderful?" but "Does it work?"

This is not a cynical or hack response. It is an attempt to judge each acting moment, each lighting setup, each cut, each music cue or sound effect, by that child standard: does it give us some tiny shard of the thrill that got us into movies in the first place?

A film is a universe where chance is never an excuse for anything, from the color of a dress to the creak of a door; it is a series of hundreds of very particular decisions, and every single one of them must be felt. That is the satisfaction and the agony of the process, and it only deepens the central mystery: given the intensely personal nature of the moviegoing experience and the completely subjective nature of the question "Does it work?" (the obvious answer being, "It works for me"), it seems almost miraculous that any two people can agree on any one of these hundreds of decisions. How is it that so much of the time people do?

It is a cliché to say that film is a collaborative medium; what that really means is that while many people can ruin a movie all by themselves, no one can make a movie work alone. Even the purest of auteur directors is limited by how well the actors and technicians realize his or her vision, and try as they might to please, the only way they can really do what the director wants is to make that vision their own. Finally, what works for the auteur must work for them.

The director can't force someone to believe something works any more than the church can make someone believe in God. People have to be persuaded. What makes the director's job easier than the missionary's (besides the fact that the director's fellow workers are paid to convert) is that unlike theology, when it comes to movies people tend to agree on what's right. One of the principal satisfactions in making movies comes from reediting or rewriting a scene for the umpteenth time and finally getting that intensely personal reaction that it works, only to discover that lo and behold everyone else involved finally thinks it works too. That feeling is intensified if someone says, "Yes, that works, but if we tweak this" —and they make a small adjustment and you immediately see that what you thought worked now works even better. That is the final proof they have made your work their own.

Clearly, agreement is often less than miraculous, but disagreements are rarely about whether something works, particularly once a film is in production. They're much more likely to be about what you want the film to do. When *All the President's Men* was about to preview, for example, we were still casting about for the right finale. The director, Alan Pakula, and Robert Redford, whose company produced the picture, were worried the ending wasn't strong enough. (In that ending, which we finally went with, reporters Bob Woodward and Carl Bernstein are back at their desks, typing away, while cannons boom to celebrate President Nixon's second inaugural; then a Teletype fills the screen, spitting out a list of Watergate convictions, ending with the terse statement "Nixon resigns.")

We all feared the film lacked closure. The problem was much discussed in the editing room, until someone—with all the back and forth it's hard to remember who—had the bright idea of cutting together the actual video footage of Nixon's abdication and tacking it on as a coda. This was wonderful stuff, with rows of servants in their white uniforms waving from White House verandas and Nixon's comic-opera palace guard rolling up the red carpet behind him as he stepped into the presidential helicopter and floated, a dim, waving figure, out of sight behind the Washington monument. No words, just the sight of Nixon's departure. It worked great. The sequence seemed to give the ending just the punch it needed.

Everyone loved it but the editor. He thought it worked, but he despised what it did. Bob Wolfe was a staunch white-shoe Republican, and he felt insulted by such palpable images of Nixon's humiliation. I pointed out that we weren't making anything up. We weren't even commenting on the facts. Millions had watched those exact shots on network TV. Wolfe called it the "boot-in-the-face" sequence. So we agreed to preview the film both ways.

First previews are a wrenching experience—something you have hacked at and played with for months, something you have seen so many times and in so many combinations that you can barely summon up any response at all, becomes the instant possession of an expectant, skeptical crowd which seems to have fierce reactions to everything. They might not know about movies, but they sure as hell know what they like.

We previewed in Denver, Bob Wolfe's way. The first fifteen minutes of the film were the stuff of sweaty palms. Dead silence. A couple of walkouts muttering angry words about a hatchet job. Surrounded by what felt like a surly mob, I suddenly saw the obvious. We had made a movie with absolutely no action at all and none of the passions most movies are about—no lust or violence but also no revenge, no family love or romance. It wasn't even much of a buddy picture. It was all talk about abstruse offscreen shenanigans.

It was as if I was seeing the film for the first time. I leaned over to Alan Pakula and whispered in his ear in a dry voice: "This is an intellectual movie." Alan's reply was immediate: "Shh, I know. Don't tell anybody." I sat rigid through the next few minutes: by God, I thought, Pakula's gone and pulled a fast one. He's slipped an intellectual movie through the system. Will there be hell to pay?

Finally, there was a bit of comic relief, one of the few light moments in the film, and the laughter washed away the threatening silence. That huddled mass out there was so gripped by the film they were looking for any release. The movie was working. I settled back to enjoy the experience along with them.

As I watched, it became clear that the audience was taking the picture more seriously than I was: their evening was at stake. They didn't want it soured by partisan politics. Republican or Democrat, much as they enjoyed the film they were constantly scanning for clues, trying to tell which side we were on. I thought ahead to the last reel, and I imagined how the audience would react if they were kicked in the face by our souped-up ending. I knew now with absolute clarity that they would feel cheated—that for them the film would collapse into an anti-Nixon diatribe, that the Nixon supporters would be insulted and the rest would get a facile boost to their self-righteousness. Either way the power of the film would be sapped; our punchy ending would knock out the picture.

The finale came up: the reporters typed, the guns boomed, the Teletype ticked. The end. I looked around and saw I wasn't the only one relieved that Bob had previewed his way the first time. Our socko ending was stowed on a high shelf in a box labeled "Boot in the Face."

I'd been forcefully reminded of something I should have known from my very first memories of watching movies: the audience was a participant—people didn't just watch, they threw themselves into the experience. They were critical and impatient, but they wanted to be allowed to enjoy the picture. They wanted in, and in a sense all we had to do was avoid giving them a reason to bail out.

There are psychological and perceptual explanations for this intense involvement. Psychologist Rudolf Arnheim years ago established that we look at paintings actively, instinctively searching for balance, for pattern, for meaning whether we're trying to or not. We are animals built to respond to the signals from our eyes as a matter of life and death. Any film editor or cameraman realizes that watching his or her work is an intuitive, visceral process—film, after all, depends on the eye collating thousands of discrete images flashing by in fractions of a second, an act beyond our conscious powers. If filmmakers haven't heard of Arnheim they still apply his principles every time they shape a scene—directing the eye with light and movement, stimulating the search for order, feeding and driving the viewer's instinctual responses.

The editor, the cameraman, the actor or actress know that the most telling criticism of their work isn't that it's phony or crude but that "it takes me out of the picture." When the audience is self-consciously examining its own responses, watching itself watch the movie, then all the razzle-dazzle in the world can't save the film. Flashy technique just becomes more stuff to look at, more proof to the audience that they're on the outside looking in. It doesn't work.

At the same time, there's the much-used comment "If they're looking at that we're in trouble." Nothing is perfect, and it requires a knowing eye to tell which weak performances, action mismatches, or lighting gaffes demand expensive correction and which will be blurred over in the sweep of events. Perhaps the greatest advantage of experience is knowing what not to worry about.

So the makers of a film pore over their materials, using all their sensitivity and all their craft to make the movie work. And the film in turn provides them with an enduring pleasure: it forces them to examine how they really see things. Seeing a moment change between set and screen, breaking it into twenty-fourths of a second, seeing it speeded up and slowed down, seeing it hundreds of times, changing it and seeing it again, seeing it in context and by itself, seeing it printed light or dark, magenta or cyan, seeing it linger in dailies with a dozen variations and flash by in the finished film, seeing it silent, with dialogue, with sound effects and music, in the presence of a nervous actor, a paying audience, and all alone, always asking what's wrong and how it could be better, creates a special bond, almost a lover's intimacy with the image.

I once watched a stark, cloudless desert sunset with a cameraman friend. He had shot a lot of sunsets; they are particularly fragile to photograph because slight changes in exposure alter the delicate hues out of all recognition. We talked about the colors while the sky darkened; he described how they slipped toward dusk. He talked for twenty minutes, calm and specific, charting the subtle pastel bands of orange, red, green chasing each other across the sky as the spectrum faded from yellow-white to purple-black. It was as if I'd never seen a sunset before. But what did I expect? This man studied sunsets for a living.

Working with film all sorts of insights, big and small, are forced on you. (Did you know, for instance, when someone stares deep into your eyes, their eyes flit back and forth every few seconds from one of your eyes to the other?) Taken as a whole, the work breeds an acute and practical awareness not just of the way we see movies but of the fundamental ways we experience the world—how we measure time, what makes something real, what moves us.

The working men and women of Hollywood may have wildly differing ideas of what they like in a movie, but they share a single overriding aim: for their film to do anything else, first and foremost it must grab and hold the audience. And whatever the aesthetic merits of Hollywood films, we must be doing something right. America has lost its dominance in steel, computer chips, even space exploration, but our films still dominate the international imagination. The appeal cannot lie entirely in the bold and brassy shine of our national culture. Our large markets at home and abroad justify lavishing time and money on our films—we have not only the will but the means to do it right, on a scale unmatched around the world. Producers might not understand all the nuances, but they spend money on Hollywood-style production because they know it brings in customers.

Art aside, Hollywood-style quality pays. Audiences want to see Hollywood movies. Why? What do we do that makes a difference? Why does it matter?

People who make movies tend to be perfectionists, but they also tend to be practical people because making movies is solving a series of very practical problems. The more successful they are, the less time they have to think about the larger theoretical issues. Making movies is too lucrative and too much fun. In this book I propose to fill that gap. I propose to look at the theoretical issues from a practical point of view, to show why quality pays, why the work works.

I believe the tools of the filmmaker's trade, the working insights and the unspoken assumptions, reveal the basic principles that give the medium such tremendous power. The day-to-day techniques of film production are signposts. Tracing back from what works can only lead to that special transaction with the screen, that thrill which makes people love movies.

Over the past twenty years I have been lucky to work around masters of the medium—writers, directors, and actors, and masters of light, sound, and film illusion—and share their struggles to make things work. I have spent months at a time staring at a blank page, or looking over someone else's shoulder while they stared at a blank page, but I've also spent months at a time on a big-budget movie set and in a studio cutting room. I have had the privilege, rare indeed for a writer in Hollywood, of following a project through as producer as well, from the idea in my head to its final release as a film. Much of my working experience has been with Alan Pakula, a director known for his meticulous craft and his fine way with actors, so many of my examples will come from his films.

I start from the working rules of thumb of my expert peers, but in the end I must rely on my own responses. I am talking about the ways we perceive the world; ultimately, the only real evidence is what works for each of us in the privacy of our minds and hearts.

What I have discovered is that we don't watch movies one way, we watch them three ways. We derive three distinct pleasures from watching a film, which I call the voyeur's, the vicarious, and the visceral. Each demands a different set of film techniques, often in contradiction with the others; each has its own sort of content, its own rules of time and space, its own way of judging reality. As we watch, the three compete within us.

Every movie is three movies running at once. Which of the three we watch, and why, is what this book is about.

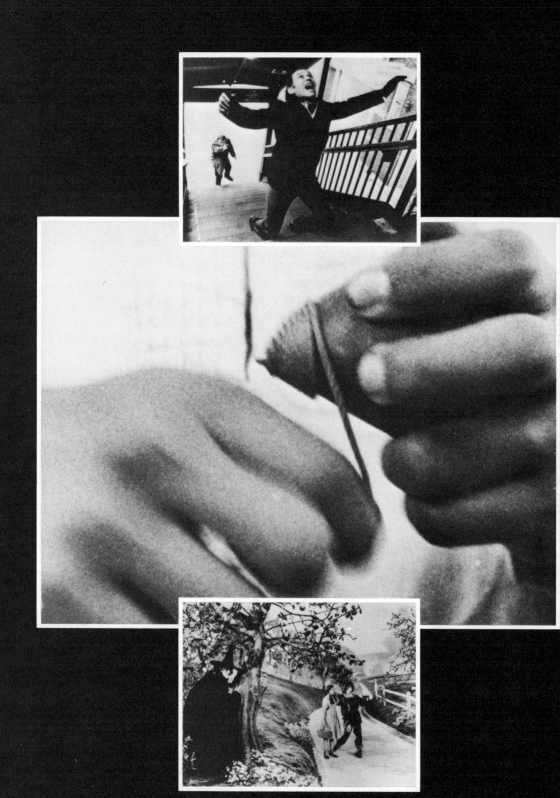

EAMES' TOYS

For a while when I was starting out in movies I worked for an authentic genius, Charles Eames. His house in the Pacific Palisades, which he designed from off-the-shelf structural steel components, was a recognized architectural classic; his furniture had been the subject of a one-man show at the Museum of Modern Art in New York; his exhibitions were world-renowned; his pioneering multiscreen films were highlights of the 1959 USIA exhibit in Moscow and the 1964 World's Fair. Eames' studio was a fantasy playground where classic bits of his design mingled with anything that captured his fancy—molded plywood splints he designed for the U.S. Navy, his prototype chairs, stunning poster-sized photos from his old exhibits stood side by side with exotic sea life, antique toys, early computer hardware, folk art. Working there you were surrounded by satisfying objects. Not exquisite in the prissy sense, but simple, practical, playful, elegant.

Charles was the same way. He always dressed in identical hazel three-piece suits, sort of the platonic ideal of the architect's rumpled corduroy, made for him at Western Costume. (They were so right, so unpretentious and impeccably made, that he never saw a reason to wear anything else.) He would move from project to project in the studio, checking out a new design for an office chair

OPPOSITE PAGE
TOP: *The French Connection*, MIDDLE: *Tops*, BOTTOM: *The Wizard of Oz*

or the layout of an exhibit on Thomas Jefferson, shooting film of a shark egg hatching. He had a remarkable eye for the enduringly beautiful. He knew what worked.

I complained to him once about my nearsightedness. With my glasses off, I said, anything more than six inches away was a blur. He seemed so interested I took off my glasses and showed him, bringing my hand up almost to my nose until I could see it. When I put on my glasses again, I saw Charles staring intently at me. "I envy you," he said. "You can get right up to things and really look at them."

Charles' idea of a good movie, however, used to drive me nuts. He was famous for a series of miniature masterpieces like *Tops* and *Toccata for Toy Trains*, scrupulously photographed celebrations of enchanting objects cut to Elmer Bernstein music. They bothered me because they weren't trying to *do* anything: they had no story, no characters, no apparent point, and for structure only a precisely felt visual logic threading through the images.

But they sure were nice to watch. Now that I am older and more relaxed about these things I can admit they worked for me, too. Charles embodied as much as any man alive the simple pleasure of looking, and his eye was so sure that if he chose to show you something you knew it was worth your attention.

In the visual swamp of our environment we are so flooded with images sucking at our consciousness it takes a Charles Eames to safely guide us. But when movies began, the world wasn't so crowded. The new wasn't old hat, and before there were stories on the screen people gathered simply to see lantern slides of strange and exotic places. Eames films are pure descendants of this tradition. Even now film still has the magical ability to take us places and show us things we've never seen before; given the right images we still respond, the way we respond to fireworks or the way small children huddle around a bug. This I call the voyeur's pleasure, by which I mean not the sexual kink but Webster's second definition of the word: the voyeur is the "prying observer." The voyeur's pleasure is the simple joy of seeing the new and the wonderful.

Eames was a painstaking craftsman. His films are gems, small but flawless. They had to be. Eames knew that although the voyeur in us wants to be amused it casts a cold eye on what it sees. It needs to be seduced. So Eames went to tremendous effort to give the voyeur's eye what it needed, a richly imagined special world, full of enticing things.

Before a world can be a special place it must actually be a world. The images on the screen can't feel like flat pictures, they must have the depth and solidity of our surroundings and must obey our everyday rules of time and space. A mundane requirement perhaps, but not a trivial one. Much of the effort of composing, lighting, and editing a film is spent creating and maintaining the illusion of a there out there. This is the bedrock beneath any Hollywood film.

The voyeur's eye is the mind's eye, not the heart's, the dispassionate observer, watching out of a kind of generic human curiosity. It is not only skeptical, it is easily bored. Eames solved this problem by changing his images often, before they lost their fresh appeal, but longer films need something else. Something has to happen. I'm not talking about plumbing depths of character or living through the thrills of a lifetime but something simpler: watching events steadily unfold in rational, explainable sequence, an engrossing story that never violates our sense of logic. This is the armature on which a Hollywood movie hangs.

These two concerns, creating a credible flow of time and space and creating a story, aren't as different as they might seem. Whether an actor crosses a room in a single step or crosses a minefield unscathed we have the same disappointed reaction. "That couldn't happen," we say. "That couldn't happen" is the ultimate criticism of the voyeur's eye. Even a film of magic and fantasy must obey its own rules or we stop suspending our disbelief.

Because the voyeur's eye bores easily, it demands surprise—so long as surprise comes with a rational explanation. Just as the voyeur's eye delights in seeing an exotic new land, it puts a premium on the clever plot twist, the arcane piece of detective work such as lifting a fingerprint from an eyeball or the obscure medical fact like the slow-acting poison that makes Edmond O'Brien a walking dead man in D.O.A.

The voyeur's eye loves to be outwitted but can't stand being duped because the voyeur's eye is as dumb as it is smart. It is a plodding, literal view of the world—it requires a thudding sense of the reality of things, of the plausibility of actions. It can ruin the most dramatic moment with the most mundane concern: "Where are they?" "How did she get in the car?" "Where did the gun come from?" "Why don't they call the police?" "He's already used six shots —how come he's still firing?" "They'd never get there in time!" For a movie to work, the voyeur's eye must be pacified. For a movie to work brilliantly, the voyeur's eye must be entranced.

CREATING A WORLD:
LIGHT, SPACE, AND SOUND

The simple pleasure of seeing is so mundane it is easy to underestimate. How much of the enjoyment of even a plot-driven melodrama like *Star Wars* comes from seeing a new world? (The much-touted café scene is a prime example.) John Ford opens *Drums Along the Mohawk* with an eighteenth-century wedding. We don't know the people yet and the words are well worn, but the house has a plain authentic feel and Ford lets the ceremony proceed at a natural pace; we're happy to watch how they tied the knot in the colonies.

On a grander scale, Francis Ford Coppola shows us the Mafia wedding in *The Godfather* and Michael Cimino the wedding in *The Deer Hunter*; David Lean gives us the trooping of the colors in *A Passage to India*; John Ford trails cavalry through the cathedral mesas of Monument Valley in his classic Westerns. Spectacle for its own sake, perhaps, but not empty images. In fact, these are the purest, least literary form of image—the image is the content. The fascination they hold, the feelings they create lie beyond words, closer to the moods of music. And in Hollywood these scenes are almost always heavily scored. This is where movie music comes into its own—where grand, sweeping themes assert themselves and embed in the viewer's consciousness.

OPPOSITE PAGE
TOP: *Star Wars*, BOTTOM:
Drums Along the Mohawk

Done right, these scenes can sum up the whole emotional experience of a film—and these are moments, don't forget, when character is virtually nonexistent, lost in the magnitude of the epic event. Films work hard to make the audience care about their characters' selfish concerns; these scenes fit the petty creatures into the larger universe, at once revealing their insignificance and making them part of something epic and grand. These moments make movies larger than life.

Eames created his worlds on a tabletop, but creating a world worth watching is usually a big job. Size is crucial. The voyeur in us must feel life encompassing the story, swallowing up the screen. We need spectacle, sweeping panorama, to convince us that the world is out there beyond the edge of the frame. Then when the filmmaker shows us smaller bits we know they aren't just what could be cobbled together, they are all the story needs.

Spectacle is the domain of the long shot, the deep-focus, wide-angle vista with a cast of thousands—impeccably outfitted, for authenticity as well as size grips the imagination. These shots are extremely expensive, often the most expensive in a movie, but the credibility they lend a film is crucial. Producers know them as "money shots"—in the double sense of big payoff and the shots where the cash is right up there on the screen. From a story point of view they are usually insignificant, but to establish a sense of place, a real world for the film, they are indispensable.

The most expensive moment in *Tucker: The Man and His Dream* (Coppola's fable about the little man who battled the moguls of Detroit), in dollars per second of screen time, is the massive gathering outside the Tucker factory the day of the "car of the future's" debut—with scores of period autos and myriad extras in period costume. The shot lasts only a few seconds, and the principals aren't even in it. The most expensive set in *Who Framed Roger Rabbit* is the period street we see for fewer than ten seconds when Benny the Car drives up. (The bulk of the scene plays on a smaller soundstage set built to match.) The most expensive single shot in *All the President's Men* is a shot of Redford changing taxicabs in front of the Kennedy Center. In terms of story, none of these moments comes close to justifying their staggering expense, yet all are money well spent and rarely affordable outside Hollywood. They give the films indispensable substance, a sense of undeniable reality beyond the screen.

And sometimes they do more. If the locale is exotic, epic shots are their own excuse. People love to be taken to a place that's like nothing they've seen before, a real-feeling place with a dense lived-in texture and a sense of evolving vitality, where the most unlikely dress and behavior are taken for granted. The strange truth of the worlds in *The Last Emperor* and *Blade Runner* provides some of the films' principal pleasures. The world itself is reason to see the film.

Here it is less important that something be absolutely real than that it feel authentic. It is the art director's job to determine just how real that is, and because authenticity is the goal the art director draws less on his or her own imagination than on broad research and experience. Art directors, like actors, aren't complimented on their originality but on their "choices."

Even the most outrageous science fiction must ring true; conversely, even the most realistic scene must be subtly altered to give the camera an undiluted sense of reality. In life, we screen out what distracts. Watching film, our eye is less forgiving. The frame implies intention. Flattened out, every part of the image takes on its true visual weight regardless of its significance. The art director must alter reality to make it feel more real on film, whether that means painting a house, planting a tree, or obscuring a sign. If the art director does the job well, his environments are a metaphor for the actions and emotions of the story. Think of the sleek, brooding feel of the Batcave in *Batman* or the jungle-rotten ruins of the Cambodian temple in *Apocalypse Now*.

LIGHT

"Light can be gentle, dreamlike, bare, living, dead, clear, misty, hot, dark, violent, springlike, falling, straight, slanting, sensual, subdued, limited, poisonous, calming and pale."

—CAMERAMAN SVEN NYKVIST

The first challenge in creating a credible world, whether it is the entire Forbidden City or Eames' toy trains, is to create a convincing space for that world to inhabit. We mustn't feel we're watching a pageant staged flat for the camera; we are looking through a window onto a three-dimensional universe, an exotic new place with all the depth and solidity of the world we already know. This is as much a problem in the chemistry and mechanics of photography as in the placement of the actors, a cameraman's problem as much as a director's. The director may layer the action in receding planes, or move people up and back, toward the camera and away into the scene rather than in flat tableau; the cameraman's problem is in many ways more subtle and demanding.

To open their screen onto another world cameramen must use all their skill to destroy its flatness. Eames, creating tiny worlds for his spinning tops or his aquarium fish, had a simple rule of thumb: to create a sense of depth, make the background lighter than the foreground (as in the pictures that open this chapter). The same rule holds for big films (note that it works for *The French Connection* and *The Wizard of Oz* as well), but for the larger canvas, for Harold Rosson shooting *The Wizard of Oz* or Gregg Toland shooting *Citizen Kane* or Gordon Willis shooting *The Godfather*, creating a sense of space requires a bigger bag of tricks.

Gordon Willis, like other cameramen, haunts art museums. Capturing three-dimensional space on a flat plane, making flat depictions of objects feel round, bathing them in atmosphere—these are problems as old as the Renaissance. There are differences be-

OVERLEAF
The money shot from *Tucker*

tween paint and film—color laws, for example, are additive for paint and subtractive for projected light (a painter mixing all his colors gets black, a cameraman gets white), but in the end, both deal only in light. Both describe how light is reflected or absorbed by objects, and both rely on how light is processed in the brain. Artists light with paint; cameramen paint with light.

A cameraman loves black blacks—they not only impart a rich dense solidity to things, they give the work an anchor, a baseline

de La Tour, *The Education of the Virgin*, RIGHT: *Barry Lyndon*

Rembrandt, *Aristotle Contemplating the Bust of Homer*, RIGHT: *The Godfather*

for the tonal changes the cameraman rings. To reproduce the much broader sensitivity of the eye within the limited palette of film, the cameraman must know exactly how little light must be put on the subject to achieve texture in the shadows and how much can be poured on and still have detail in the highlights. The good cameramen use the full range of their medium, keeping a scene dark save for a single brilliant highlight or juxtaposing a dark scene with a hot, overexposed one.

Light defines objects; their relation to each other and the space they occupy is described by the light that etches them. If this light comes from an identifiable source—if it comes from one direction and is explained by a bright window, say, or an overhead lamp—it acts as a unifying force, spreading over its world in a way we recognize, its highlight and shadow telling us where each element resides. Rembrandt and Leonardo are masters of directed light (though we don't see the source); so are Caravaggio and Georges de La Tour. Vermeer adds a layer of subtlety with his fine sense of how light enters a room and infuses the shadows with a reflected glow; Monet's twilight paintings go a step further, imbuing the air itself with the dense luminescence of sunset bouncing in the mist.

Surprisingly, cameramen say that color is easier to shoot than black and white. When the cameraman sets out to create a world, the first problem is to create a sense of depth on a flat plane. This is really a problem in separation: he has to make his subjects stand out from the background and appear to overlap rather than blend into each other. Shooting black and white, the cameraman has only various tones of gray to work with. He or she can put the brightly lit side of an actress' face against a shadowy background, for instance, or can outline her with a specially placed backlight called a liner. Shooting color, however, the cameraman can rely on hue— a pink and a blue that would read as identical grays will stand out clearly from each other, even if they are both lit without highlights or shadows. So the task is simplified. But the good cameraman never forgets the lessons of the painters—that while layering creates depth, layering alone doesn't define space. For that, objects need their own tangible sense of volume, of size and weight, and in color or black and white that means sculpting them with light and shadow. In the words of cameraman Eric Saarinen, "The key to composition is 'light-dark-light.' "

While color separates, it also unifies. Art directors choose the color of every costume and every setting to pull a scene together, to create a dominant mood, to give a sense of completeness to the whole film; cameramen choose a particular color of light for the same reasons. During shooting they carefully control the color temperature of their light to create a yellow-warm or bluish-cold look; then, when the film is all but done, they return for the final step in finishing the film, color-correcting (or "timing") the print. No two scenes in a film will have identical color. Even if the same kind of film stock is used for the whole movie, every production run of that stock is slightly different, every processing bath, each lens has a slightly different color cast; the cameraman has been less than perfect in lighting and exposing every shot. Now, as the lab tries to make its first print of the finished film from the negative, the cameraman has a final chance to adjust the color and brightness of every scene so that all the shots made under all the different conditions feel like a consistent whole.

A film lab looks and smells like what it is, a chemical factory. The elite of the factory hands are the film timers, technicians with an artist's eye, experts who know exactly what will happen if they add small increments of different-colored light when the film is printed. The cameraman will sit with a timer in a dark cubicle, running the film shot by shot and discussing how the brightness and color balance in each scene need adjustment. Current technology has them looking at an especially calibrated television monitor, adjusting the color as you would at home, though they know the monitor gives only a rough idea of what they'll get on film.

This can be a very tricky task. If a shot is underexposed, do you lighten it so the whites match, even if the blacks go milky-gray? If a scene plays under red light, the first cut to normal light will look green to the eye. Do you pink it up? The timer must not only know the eye's tricks, but he or she must be able to understand the cameraman's intention and have the technique to carry it through. Cameramen know that a good timer can make them look better and a bad timer can ruin their work; the best timers are a prized commodity at the lab, like star ball players, a major asset in selling their company's services to the cameraman.

Just as important to the cameraman as the color of light is its consistency. Liquid light, light that looks as if it has been poured over objects, cameramen call soft light. It is the beloved north light of painters. It caresses people, fading gently into rich shadows, imparting the solid, sensual roundness of a Leonardo Madonna. As painters have long known, it is the perfect light to create three-dimensional forms and anchor them in space. But for film, soft light long posed a problem: its very softness comes from its disper-

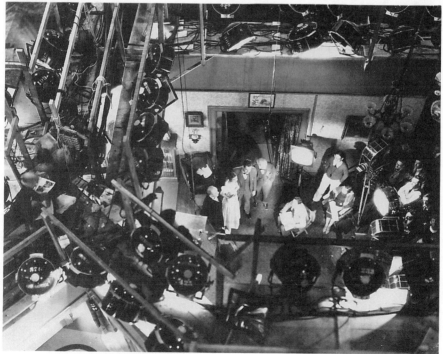

sal, its weakness. Soft light comes not from a single point but from a spread-out source like the north sky. In the very early days, when films were shot on open-air sets, the sky could provide the source. But once film moved indoors and sets were lit by electricity, soft light had to be made by pushing lamplight through diffusion material or bouncing it off reflectors to spread it out, and both dimmed its brilliance beyond the early capabilities of film. So cameramen had to work with the naked lights, each one a pinpoint source, carving hard-edged ebony shadows: hard light. Not the single soft caress of the open sky but the contrasting glare of a dozen mini-suns.

The shadows cause the problems. Our eye has great latitude—no matter how sunny the day we can always see into the shadow areas, even on a ski slope or a white-sand beach. To a film emulsion, though, someone standing in the sun might as well be an astronaut standing in the harsh light of the moon's surface. Direct sunlight is so much brighter than the shadows that film emulsion does not have the latitude to register detail in both at once. If a face is photographed in direct sunlight and the film is exposed to show details in the sunny areas, every lump in the complexion casts a dark pit of a shadow and the lee side of the nose is a great black hole. Outdoors, mirrored reflectors can bounce sunlight into the shadows. Inside, when film needed the candlepower, cameramen used hard lights and then filled the shadows with secondary lights. These created secondary shadows which demanded still more lights if the cameraman wasn't careful.

Tuning this lighting is a demanding skill. On the set, scenes look flat and bright; only filtered through the limited sensitivity of film emulsion do they take on their full range of tones. (That little monocle cameramen wear around their neck is a piece of precisely smoked glass. When they peer through it, the darkened image gives them a better idea of what the film will see.)

But hard light has its own satisfactions. Used sparingly it can add a sense of drama, of eyeless sockets in cavernous faces, of men lurking beyond the glare of street lamps, of faces slashed by light knifing through the slats of a venetian blind. It is the light that put the "noir" in "film noir." Used in profusion, hard light can lend a scene a glossy sheen, a sense of being brighter and sharper and shinier than reality. The glamour of the thirties was drenched in hard light.

But while hard light paints powerful images, it is an intractable way to create the normal play of light and shade away from the

James Wong Howe shooting *The Adventures of Tom Sawyer* (1938)

OPPOSITE PAGE
Marlene Dietrich
in hard light

9000-watt Molequartz®
Nine-light Molepar®

sun's glare. It requires surpassing skill and a heavy investment of time to adjust the many lights while avoiding unnatural multiple shadows. You have to use all your artifice to imitate nature because you can't do it nature's way.

In the late sixties, as lenses and film stocks became more sensitive and lighting technology evolved powerful new sources, the quartz-halogen lamp and the "nine-light array," cameramen led by Vilmos Zsigmond (*McCabe and Mrs. Miller*), Haskell Wexler (*The Thomas Crown Affair*), Vittorio Sterraro (*The Conformist*), and Gordon Willis (*Klute* and *The Godfather*) could borrow more freely from the painters. Unlike the sky soft light of the early days, when interiors were shot outside under muslin, this light could be manipulated, varied in direction and intensity. What was once an occasional effect became an efficient way of making pictures. Color films took on a new depth and glow, and the cameramen pushed the lower limits of film sensitivity. This new directed soft light allowed lighting to have a natural feel, to wrap around objects and fill in its own shadows; it allowed for rooms to be lit by window light and for light sources to mix and blend the way they do in life.

Even before soft light became practical, the great cameramen honored directed light, and with their mastery they created the same complex texture of reality. But now what only the greats could once achieve we take as commonplace. Even in good television we expect a room will be lit by daylight pouring through the windows and bouncing around as in a painting by Vermeer, creating a rich and vivid space.

Soft versus hard
LEFT: *The Godfather*, RIGHT:
Sunset Boulevard

SPACE

To the voyeur's eye, a change of camera angle is a serious event. A cut from one shot to another not only breaks flow, it leaps us from one place to another, forcing us to get our bearings anew within the movie space. Done wrong, this can be a very disorienting experience. It is the editor's job to make these moves invisible; like the cameraman the editor must create a space so solid and convincing that the viewer never feels lost or confused. The editor has to make us feel comfortable that we know, without ever thinking about it, where our actors are and how they face off. Are they looking at each other? If one is speaking, is the other one in earshot? Where are they in the room?

While making cuts, the editor is constantly constrained by the apparent realities of the cameraman's space. The cameraman creates a world, the editor lives within it. If a cameraman gives a scene a strong sense of the source and direction of its light, for example, it is that much easier for the editor to jump around the room—if we leap to a close-up washed in bright highlights, for instance (what a cameraman would call "over key"), we assume the person is near the window; if we then cut to another close-up, lit just as brightly but from the other side, we assume the second person is also close to the window but facing the first.

We rely on these lighting cues more than you might realize. Occasionally, a strong-willed star with a window on her left is convinced her face only looks good lit from the right. The diplomatic or lucky cameraman might be able to have her trade places with her partner, who is lit from the other side by the window; otherwise the cameraman will be forced to "switch keys"—that is, fake it and light her as if the window were on her right anyway. The star will praise the cameraman when she sees the dailies, but the editor will damn him because in spite of all the other clues in the scene, when the editor cuts the scene together the viewer will feel, in some unsettling way, that the two people are facing the same direction instead of facing each other. A brilliant cameraman can light the star just right, maybe bring in some other strong visual clue and get away with it. But it will cause him sleepless nights.

The editor has to uphold not just the integrity of the cameraman's space but the integrity of the actors' behavior. He or she has to make sure they obey the basic laws of time and space. We have to trust that the cigarette an actress lights in one shot is burning when we cut to a different angle ten seconds later (with ten seconds' worth of ash), that her cup of coffee doesn't magically empty, her hair doesn't rearrange itself, her eyeglasses don't pop on and off untouched by human hands. These concerns of "continuity," as they're called, may seem trivial, but they dominate the editor's every decision. The thread of reality must be unbroken or we won't fully give ourselves up to the screen. Our voyeur's eye will set off alarms, and the editor will have committed the gravest of sins: the editor will have pulled us out of the picture.

There is no such thing as perfect continuity, of course. Since every shot is distinct, sometimes filmed out of order, often taken hours or days apart, it is impossible for minute details to match exactly. The expertise of the script supervisor (who is responsible for continuity on the set) as well as the hairdresser, costumer, prop master, and art director is as much to know what won't matter as to catch what will. Must the director retake a shot, perhaps brilliantly acted, because the actor had the cigarette in his right hand instead of his left? Or is the viewer's eye somewhere else, his mind distracted by the emotion, the flaw blurred by the rush of action? Should the editor use the take that matches action or the one with a stronger performance? Is it true, in the refrain of the editing

The glass leaps into Ingrid Bergman's hand in these two adjoining frames from *Notorious*. The passing waiter helps to mask the mismatch.

room, "If they're looking at that, we're in trouble"?

Matching is the most obvious continuity problem but not the most disorienting. A sure sign of a neophyte director is a film that is all tight close-ups punctuated by panoramic long shots. Graphically, close-ups and long shots are easier to design and almost always more visually satisfying than the prosaic medium shot. They look better through the viewfinder. Long shots can be composed with a painter's eye for landscape or tableau, while close-ups make for strong compositions—shallow focus at closer distances blurs the background so it doesn't compete with the strong graphics of the face. But while the long shots and close-ups may be handsome, they don't tell a story. Panoramic long shots put us too far away from the actors to read their behavior; tight close-ups not only overpower all but the most crucial moments, they isolate the character and disorient the viewer. Where is this head, floating among colorful out-of-focus blobs? How far is he from the people he's talking to? Where are they?

In conventional editing, the editor opens with a master shot, the broad angle of spectacle, to ground us and orient the scene, and then jumps into closer angles to tell the story. But not only must

How lenses affect space:
The telephoto lens pushes
the kids together. The wide
angle pulls them apart.

the closer angles tell the story, when the editor shifts angles the spatial geometry must hold. Since perception of space changes with distance, with the focal length of the lens and the angle between the camera and the subject (whether the camera is high or low, facing the actor or looking at his profile), much of the cameraman's art is to re-create the apparent reality of the master by altering the relationships in the closer angles. Often what feels like artifice on the set looks more real on film. "Cheat toward the camera" is a common refrain to the actor—look more full into the camera, look away from the actress you are talking to so the audience will believe you are really facing her.

To maintain the integrity of the space, the cameraman must choose matching angles. If two characters are talking, a three-quarter view of one and a full face of the other will raise a question in the viewer's mind that requires explanation. Why are we looking full into one face and at the side of another? There can be good reasons—we might be watching the scene from the point of view of a third party, for instance, or one of the characters might be hiding his face from the other—but if it is done arbitrarily, the space distorts. We spend our mental energy wondering where the characters are. And for the cameraman, space comes first. He must protect the reality of his world.

While everyone who makes movies appreciates the visual tour de force, it is a given in Hollywood that "anything that makes you conscious of the camera pulls you out of the picture." A clumsy camera move is obviously distracting, but even an astonishingly beautiful camera move can be a distinct liability. If we are appreciating fancy camera moves we are no longer involved in the world behind the screen. Our minds are on the brilliance of the technicians and off the story they are trying to tell.

This is not to say the camera cannot be used expressively, but when it is done well, in films like *Citizen Kane* and *Psycho*, the style so matches the content that it feels like the natural choice. This is a much more difficult task than throwing something eye-popping on the screen. The visual power of *Citizen Kane* lies not in the pizzazz of the camera work but in the way it enhances the emotional impact of the film, the way it serves the story. Much of the audience probably doesn't notice there is anything stylistically spectacular about it. A twelve-year-old can watch the shower sequence in *Psycho* and relish the terror without noticing how it's made.

This is just as true in mundane scenes as in the grand moment. Cameras are usually on movable dollies, and camera operators are constantly making invisible adjustments in the frame to accommodate the action; keeping the small moves invisible is a fine skill. In Hollywood, the camera operator works for the cameraman, following precise instructions for framing the scene, but a good camera operator is as much artist as technician, and a good dolly grip (the person who actually pushes the camera) is highly valued—together they have to sense the action and blend their movements in a delicate dance so their adjustments feel like an organic response to the actors' moves rather than an arbitrary relocation, even while they're subtly anticipating what the audience will want to see.

Cameramen evolve their own rules for what they think will or won't pull the audience out of the picture. Gordon Willis doesn't like to lower his camera on its hydraulic arm, for instance, when a character sits. He'll tilt the camera, but arming down he feels draws too much attention to the move. And like most serious cameramen he will never willingly use a naked zoom—that is, he will not simply zoom his camera in on something without covering the zoom effect with another camera move. Zooming appears to bring us closer by increasing the focal length of the lens; we begin by watching through a wide angle and end up watching through a telephoto. That changes the optical qualities of the shot—in telephoto shots, planes stack up on top of each other and backgrounds can go out of focus.

It is much easier to zoom in on something than actually move the camera, which involves laying track, dolly grips, and all the physical problems of moving four hundred pounds of camera, dolly, and operator through space, but the eye is never really fooled by a zoom. We don't feel that we have moved closer, we only feel we are watching through binoculars. Suddenly we are conscious of the optical mechanics of watching a movie. Zooms are constantly abused on television, where tight shooting schedules preclude more time-consuming techniques.

While cameramen consider zooms in the wrong place a criminal offense, even Willis uses them when he can fold them in invisibly, if the camera is moving in a certain way, or perhaps to give a subliminal jolt, as in the scene in *All the President's Men* when Redford thinks he's being followed and starts to run down an empty street. Willis tracks with him—when Redford turns suddenly to look behind him, Willis zooms the camera into close-up. It feels like the end of the tracking move, with a little extra bite. It took half a dozen takes to get it right.

Keeping the audience in the picture is the cameraman's constant concern, even in the most ordinary scene. Consider two people talking while driving in a car. Cameramen do not like to shoot this scene. It is almost impossible to come up with something new, and most of the old solutions give cameramen hives. In the first place, the cameraman is severely constrained. There is no room to maneuver; unless the camera is put in the backseat and photographs the back of the actors' heads the cameraman has to build a camera mount outside the car. Where?

The cameraman and the director must make a basic choice: do they want the audience to be inside the car with the actors or outside the car looking in? To make viewers feel as if they are inside, there are only three angles to use—straight from the sides through either of the two side windows or straight from the front through the windshield. But it is not enough to shoot inside the window

frames—a lens whose focal length makes us feel as if the camera is inside the car must be used. Too long a focal length, and we will feel we are watching a car from the outside with the glass removed. If the director doesn't mind the feeling that we are outside the car, which tends to distance us from the characters and pull us out of the picture, the cameraman's choices are greater, but not much.

In spite of the storytelling advantages, we rarely see a film anymore where the front windshield is removed. When car shots were done on sound stages in front of rear-projection screens, removing the windshield was a simple matter (easier than artificially creating the proper reflections), but now that such shots are done outside, on the road, removing the glass is unworkable since we would see the wind in the driver's face. Practical considerations have made shooting through the front windshield a convention of modern films, and perforce audiences have come to accept it, though filmmakers know it is an uneasy compromise and for important dialogue scenes try to choose another angle.

But any one angle is usually not enough. If the scene is important, and the director wants control in the editing room over performance and pace, he or she will require not only a master shot (or "two-shot") of both actors but close "single" shots on each actor as well, to select the best performance of each separately and shorten the scene if necessary by cutting out parts of it when switching angles.

Now the cameraman's troubles are compounded. If the driver is shot from one side of the car and the rider from the other, as would seem natural, the cameraman creates an instant problem. On-screen, the driver will be facing one way—right, say, with the background whizzing along right-to-left behind him—and the passenger will be facing the other—in this case, looking left with the background whizzing along left-to-right behind him. While intellectually we know the two are in the same car, the visual effect is disorienting, as if they didn't share the same front seat but were traveling in opposite directions. Skilled cameramen can minimize the problem, but they know they are essentially dealing with damage control. Lucky is the director who can put the characters in the back of a chauffeured limousine and shoot more or less from the front seat.

When the evidence of our eyes conflicts with what we know to be true, we have to ignore what we see; this takes conscious effort, which pulls us out of the picture, and it makes us mistrust the filmmakers. It plants a seed of doubt, which can sprout roots that crack apart a scene. Even the simplest of scenes becomes a nightmare of disorientation, for instance, if the cameraman "crosses the line."

Usually, when two people are talking they are facing each other. But merely because two people are facing each other in reality doesn't mean it will look that way on film. In order for actors in separate close-ups to appear face-to-face, they must be photographed looking in opposite directions: one must be photographed looking left-to-right, and the other must look right-to-left. If they aren't, the effect is quite remarkable—an actor can be looking almost dead into the camera, ever so subtly to one side, but if it's the wrong side we won't feel he's facing his partner.

Cameramen and script supervisors (who are usually the final arbiters of crossing the line on the set) discovered that in most cases

they could achieve the face-to-face effect if, when the camera shoots both actors, it keeps to one side of a line drawn from nose to nose. If the camera strays over that line and shoots the actors from different sides, they will appear on-screen to be facing the same direction, not talking to each other but to some invisible third character.

Sorting out the "sight lines," as they are called, is a piece of arcanum which holds directors in thrall to their directors of photog-

The dinner table
conundrum

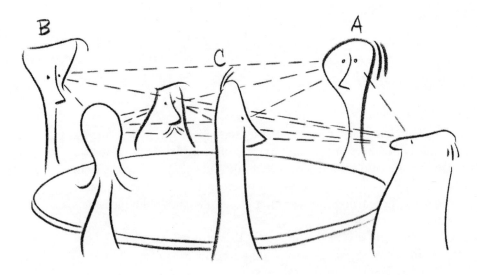

raphy, enchained by manifold diagrams scribbled on the backs of envelopes, and cameramen, more than they would like to admit, in thrall to their script supervisors. In a static scene between two people it's a trivial problem—just keep the camera on the same side of the actors. But what if the actors are moving? What if there are three, four, or five actors?

Thus, cameramen find dinner-table scenes among the hardest to shoot. Every actor shares a sight line with every other actor at the table; if the editor were to demand absolute freedom to cut at will from one actor to another in the editing room, the cameraman would have to shoot dozens of angles. As it is, the cameraman prays the director has a very clear plan of the order in which to move from actor to actor when the scene is cut and gives the director angles with sight lines to match that sequence. Later, if the scene needs to be cut differently, the cameraman's name will be a curse on the editor's lips. (Best of all for the cameraman, the director can deal with the problem as Woody Allen does in *Hannah and Her Sisters* and shoot the scene in one continuous take with the camera circling the table. Then the editor has to use that one whole shot, unbroken, or none at all.)

SOUND

Close your eyes and your ears will still tell you where you are—indoors or outdoors, in the wilderness or in a backyard or on a street, in an empty church or a busy office, a kitchen or a prison. How much of the frenzy of a trading room comes from the frantic yelling, how much of the calm of a church from its sepulchral silence?

I remember an odd experience, listening to a piano concerto from the cheap seats at the Hollywood Bowl. It was like watching a ball game from the center-field bleachers—I could make out only gross body movements. Luckily, I was watching a flamboyant performer, but the more he flailed away, the more uncomfortable I became, until I realized the problem: I was so far away I was hearing silence when he hit the keys and crescendos when his hands were lifted dramatically in the air.

Usually, we don't even bother to distinguish between the cues that come from our eyes and our ears because, after all, they are a perfect match and perfectly synchronous. But in making a film, capturing sound and image are two entirely different processes. Not only do they not automatically fit, it takes a great deal of effort to bring them together in just the right mix. But our voyeur's ear demands it. When our senses reinforce each other they create a compelling reality; when our senses conflict we tend to trust our eyes (if we don't laugh), but the glories lavished on our eyes are tarnished. If I see a pit bull leaping at me from the screen and hear a kitten's purr, I'll laugh, but how much less terrifying is the pit bull if he is given the barks of a German shepherd or if the barking sounds are muddied and distorted by poor recording or they don't quite match his snarls?

Some student films approach the Hollywood film for visual polish, but I've never seen one that doesn't betray its origins in the sound track. Most other countries don't show our exaggerated respect for sound—in Italy or India, for instance, directors routinely shoot silent and add sound later, crudely but efficiently. They don't need soundproof studios or superquiet cameras, they don't have to shoot more takes because the sound wasn't right. But here in America most scenes are shot and recorded simultaneously, at considerably more trouble and expense, to get that extra correspondence between the visual and aural; here film workers consider a good sound job to be the acid test of a first-rate professional film.

Film is edited in two parts, a picture reel and a carefully synchronized matching reel of sprocketed magnetic sound film. Toward the end of the editing process, when the exact sequence and length of shots is accepted as final, the sound editors take over. Their job is to give the sound vivid, consistent, convincing "reality." They pull apart the rough sound track. The different bits of dialogue are separated so they can be rerecorded later to smooth differences in sound perspective, recording levels, and mike timbre. The editors pore over every chance sound, assessing it, replacing it if it doesn't ring true.

Synchronous dialogue almost always sounds more convincing than dialogue added later because subtle differences in performance are reflected in the actor's voice as well as his demeanor. But with other sounds the opposite is usually the case. The laws of sound recording are such that a well-recorded voice usually results in poorly recorded background sounds. The actual background sounds—that is, the sounds as picked up by a microphone and recorded on tape—just don't sound "real." They can be too loud, too harsh, too muddy, or inaudible (I remember doing a film about the making of a lithograph and adding a sound for talc being sprinkled on the stone). Usually, almost every sound effect is replaced— every door slam, car start, key jangle, pouring liquid, paper rustle.

OPPOSITE PAGE
Eleanor Counts, dancer, gets her break supplying the footsteps for the dead chimpanzee actor Jiggs in *Her Jungle Love* (1938).

Footsteps are added, augmented, or deleted to match the sense of the picture. In fact, one of the hardest decisions is when to use footsteps—sometimes it seems they are indispensable, at other times an annoying distraction.

Whole sound settings are built, layer by layer. When a scene is being shot, the sound recordist makes the crew stand immobile while he records the sound of silence. Editors then build endless loops of this "presence," or "room tone," as an underlying constant for the track, the barely audible background hum which defines a space. On top of that they create whole environments out of ambient sound, turning a silent stage into a noisy tenement, for example, with babies squealing and TVs playing through the thin walls, subways passing underneath, arguments rising from the street. They might add closer sounds on top—the electric hum of a refrigerator, the tick of a clock, the drip of a faucet. A good sound job can require as many as fifteen or twenty reels of "foley effects" (the footsteps, paper rustles, key jingles that match the action we see on the screen) and another forty reels of more generalized background sounds going at once. Editors can compose virtual symphonies of sound effects, more felt than heard by the audience, in support of the image.

Finding just the right sound can be as exacting a task as finding just the right image. *All the President's Men* opens with huge typewriter keys, bigger than the screen, pounding out a date, a visual metaphor for the power of the press. They demanded a special

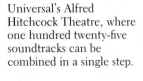

Universal's Alfred Hitchcock Theatre, where one hundred twenty-five soundtracks can be combined in a single step.

sound, as much larger than life as they were. The sound editor overlaid key hits from a carefully chosen typewriter (he tried half a dozen machines) with the attack sound, the front end, of whip cracks, and the decay sound, the back end, of cannon shots; the mixer took almost four hours to blend them. For *It's a Mad Mad Mad Mad World* Stanley Kramer is said to have sent his effects editor to a gas station halfway to Palm Springs to record a squeaky men's room door because it was the perfect sound for the squeaky wheel on Terry-Thomas' banged-up jeep. Sound editors are connoisseurs of aural tidbits, which they store in large libraries—Chic Ciccolini, for instance, one of the premier sound editors in New York, has a baby cry he's particularly proud of and a deliciously evocative recording of a distant car full of teenagers driving over a manhole cover. They've starred in many sound tracks mixed on the East Coast.

As any concertgoer knows, space colors sound. Though sound editors can do wonders, they cannot change the fundamental quality of the sound they are given. Every place has its particular ambience, its blend of absorption and echo which emphasizes certain frequencies, creates certain assumptions of size and mood. If the sound editors are given something recorded in a closet, they can't make it sound as if it were taped in a church, though they might be asked to if forced to replace unacceptable dialogue tracks in the editing, and, indeed, a sophisticated technology exists to help them. They can make a close approximation, but you will hear the difference. Even today, with digital technology and computer-enhanced sound, there is only so much they can fake electronically. In fact, the best way to achieve a larger acoustical effect is still to play the closet track in a large, resonant space and rerecord it from a distance. Sound is too elusive, too complicated to manipulate freely. As the picture editor is at the mercy of the camerman, the sound editor is at the mercy of the sound recordist.

Sound has its own laws of perspective. Closer sounds are more "present"—they contain a wider range of frequencies, particularly highs. A good sound recordist looks through the camera not only to tell where it's safe to put the mikes but also to judge the size of the shot; the sound must feel the same size. This is a tricky judgment, depending on the ambience, background noise, and type of mike, but generally the mike must be markedly closer than the camera to match picture perspective.

The job of recording is complicated by what is called "the cocktail party effect." Your ear has a nose for news. It will pick out an important sound—a conversation in which your name is mentioned, for instance—from a mass of equally loud noise; it will focus on it and blot out the distractions in a remarkable feat of echolocation and spatial imaging. When the same sounds are recorded and played back through a speaker, however, the spatial clues no longer exist and it all sounds like mush. Part of the recordist's job is to know how the sound on the set will translate onto the theater's speakers, and one reason badly recorded films sound bad is because the recordist let himself be fooled. For movie sound to sound right, it has to be closer and cleaner than the real sound. But not too close or too clean.

On the face of it, stereo sound presents exciting possibilities. Now that sound can have another spatial dimension, won't it enlarge the movie experience, envelop the audience even more? Yes and no. Well-mixed stereo creates a sense not just of breadth but of depth, and that is all to the good. Subtly used, stereo can enhance the feeling of a solid, dimensional world behind the screen. But it has strict limitations.

Consider Cleopatra's leap. Elizabeth Taylor's 1963 *Cleopatra* was one of the first films with multichannel sound. I remember the thrill of watching Liz pace her cavernous palace, declaiming petulantly, her shrill voice tracking with her across the enormous screen of the Egyptian Theater in Hollywood. The movie is very conservatively shot, without a lot of jumping around, but in one scene the cameraman got clever and let Liz slip screen-right to balance out his composition, only to have her pop up screen-left in the very next shot, in the middle of the same speech. She was so securely placed on the right side by her voice that when the cut came she seemed to leap thirty feet across the screen. I could accept the visual jump —it happens frequently—but somehow the precise sound pinned her to the screen like a butterfly on a mounting board. Sound mixers are aware of this problem, and, unless the cutting patterns allow them to keep their aural space consistent, they tend to use stereo imaging only for specific effects, like shock sounds or the menace of approaching helicopters. Dialogue stays on the center track. In an odd way, aural space is more rigid than visual space.

Now that speakers encircle the theater, aural space is also more all-enveloping. With the advent of surround-sound the choppers are behind you. This technique can be very effective (think of the air cavalry in *Apocalypse Now* and the cheering crowds in *Woodstock*), but it is even more prone to misuse than stereo. It is one thing to have the world behind the window of the screen enlarged, deepened, expanded; it is quite another to destroy the effect of the window altogether.

Our conventions work within the limits of the screen; unless we are making a film whose subject is those very limits, the way some modern painting is about painting, we need the frame to define our scope and to reassure our audience, just as painters do. Experimental films may try to make the audience conscious of film conventions, to confront the audience with its own limitations and the limitations of the medium, but Hollywood films need the comfort of the frame to work their magic.

Hollywood technique, no matter how flamboyant, at its best prides itself on being invisible, on serving the story. "If you're admiring the work," the saying goes, "it's not working." You've been pulled out of the picture. The sound of choppers roaring up behind us doesn't put us in the screen so much as make us conscious of the serried rows of blackness, the glowing exit signs in the back of the hall. It makes the screen look smaller.

People want to believe in the magical space behind the screen, and audiences are willing to excuse a lot of sloppy work to give themselves up to the illusion. But Hollywood technique is based on the faith that the audience is more demanding than it knows, that subtleties invisible to the viewer make a crucial difference to the viewing experience. This is never truer than when it comes to maintaining a consistent movie space. Even Alfred Hitchcock, who loved tricking the audience as much as anyone, was meticulous in this regard. His characters may be hanging off the torch of the Statue of Liberty or Lincoln's nose on Mount Rushmore, but they are precisely placed in a concrete, credible world respecting the laws of dimensional space. Hitchcock knew that his tricks worked best on an audience that felt solidly grounded, that had settled comfortably into his grasp. The solidity of his world was the foundation on which Hitchcock built the more elaborate involvements of his art.

MOVIE TIME

The voyeur's pleasure—the pleasure of simply watching, of looking for its own sake—is in a sense the most primitive of movie pleasures. Moments of movie spectacle, long on imagery and short on words, echo the simple enumerative power of a classic picture book for very young children. As with a two-year-old, it is enough for us to look at the pictures.

Goodnight Moon, for example, a book by Margaret Wise Brown that has captivated two-year-olds for forty years, shows a picture of a cozy bedroom and then page by page says goodnight to everything in it:

Goodnight Moon

Goodnight clocks
And goodnight socks

Goodnight little house
And goodnight mouse

Goodnight comb
And goodnight brush

Goodnight nobody
Goodnight mush

And goodnight to the old lady
whispering "hush"

Not exactly *The Iliad*, but exercising its own fascination. Yet even in *Goodnight Moon* the single picture isn't enough. Even without characters or a plot there have to be pages to turn. And if you have ever read to a two-year-old you know you must keep them turning. This lesson is easily lost when it comes to film. Epic scenes are so expensive and so much trouble to achieve that it is hard to resist the desire to get your money's worth by lingering.

First cuts are usually very long on spectacle. Only as the film is whittled down from its first sodden mass does the maker come to the painful conclusion that these most elaborate of scenes quickly wear out their welcome. The truth is we love to watch them—for fifteen, maybe thirty seconds. Then we're asking, "What next?"

(The endless twenty-minute wedding party in *The Deer Hunter* comes to mind.) Spectacle must be tossed off, it seems, almost thrown away, to be most effective, so the audience senses there is life offscreen, so the audience feels it is being shown what the filmmakers have chosen rather than everything they've got.

On the simplest possible level, images fascinate us—and then we get bored. We need to move on. Eames solved the problem on his micro scale with a rapid succession of images propelled along by music. On a larger scale, of course, filmmakers rely on story, what E. M. Forster called the "and then . . . and then." Things have to keep happening. The child in us that loves a story demands we turn the page.

People bore easily, but they have a compensating virtue: they are relentlessly optimistic. They will hang in there beyond all reason, hoping something better will come along, as long as things keep coming. Hollywood movies are particularly afraid of boring people so they are particularly adept at sustaining people's hope. One secret of their success worldwide, I'm convinced, is their relentless pace.

Movies are closer to music than to other visual media in that they're so strongly time-driven. A play unfolds at the director's pace, but we choose where to look; filmmakers force us to watch a precisely chosen image for an exact length of time. It is a miracle, when one thinks about it, that we can sit still for anyone else's rhythms, but we not only sit still, we revel in them. That is the glory and the burden of film.

Directors and editors are keenly aware of their power and their responsibility. Together they pore over screen moments, refining them by fractions of a second. A well-edited movie has been built up and stripped down dozens of times, until the story is there just so—nothing superfluous, nothing left out, nothing too short or too long. No fat, or rather the editor has massaged the fat, sensing when the curves are exactly right. I have known an editor to spend four hours refining a single splice. Sometimes one frame does make a difference.

Just as space is altered when it's flattened against a screen, so is time. Somehow we have more patience with a live person in the room than with a huge face light-sprayed on a wall, and once action is two-dimensional we get it quicker, just as we absorb a flat image quicker than we absorb a three-dimensional space. Most plays fail as films not because they are too "small" and need to be "opened up" but because they are too slow. They need to be sped up. A playwright once said that so much happens in a movie that he could write a whole play about what goes on in the space between two movie scenes.

The art of editing is in large part sensing this difference—feeling how much less of something is required on the screen, feeling that edge where we teeter into boredom. There is no formula for this. It is a function of many variables—the editor's internal clock, the exact composition of the shot, what precedes and follows it, the overall rhythms of the film, even the size of the screen.

As Rudolf Arnheim pointed out, movies are a fundamentally different experience from television because when we watch the small TV screen our eyes lock onto the image and when we watch a big screen we're forced to scan back and forth to take it all in. Locking-in is a passive response (it seems to induce an alpha state, like meditation); scanning is active.

When you are scanning an image your eye takes time to find what it is looking for. Each new cut takes an instant to register. Editors play with that time: because wide master shots take longer to absorb, they leave them on for a fraction longer before starting important action; in action sequences they shorten that instant by using the movement in one shot to lead your eye to the right spot in the next (so-called center of interest editing). Though editors work on small-screen editing machines, they periodically project their films theater-size to double-check themselves.

Overall, when we watch movies, at least Hollywood movies, our voyeur's eye demands a pace faster than life. Whether this condition is fundamental to the medium or something filmmakers have created by exploiting the advantages of film over real life is an unanswerable question. But part of the satisfaction of Hollywood films, even the most realistic, is their streamlined version of reality. Things work smoother on an almost subliminal level. In movies people don't waste time looking for parking places or making change, and the audience knows it. If an actor can't find a parking place, the audience expects his bumbling to affect the story; if it doesn't, the filmmakers have slowed the pace for nothing and loosened their grip on the viewer. They have wasted time. And the most valuable commodity to the Hollywood filmmaker isn't sets or stars or shooting days. It's screen time.

The demands of spectacle fight the demands of pace. Directors usually use wide master shots as transitions between scenes to establish a new place and situate their characters. These "establishing shots" are often otherwise pointless depictions of actors walking up to buildings, climbing stairs, entering rooms. Cameramen call them "shoe leather" and don't much enjoy shooting them because they have the nagging suspicion they will never end up in the film. Perhaps three quarters of the time they are right; all too often these shots deaden the pace too much to use. The problem, as the director knows, is that the other 25 percent of the time they are absolutely essential, and you can't predict which 25 percent you will need.

Gordon Willis and Alan Pakula addressed a particularly intractable case in *The Parallax View*, a Warren Beatty thriller shot from a half-finished script during a writers' strike. Sure that the film would be transformed in the editing room, Willis shot what he called a "jump-cut movie" that would let the director and the editor reshape the scenes and reorganize them without the glue of transitional masters. He matched his close-ups, using a fixed selection of head sizes for most scenes so that even with the shoe leather cut out the visual architecture of the story would hold—the viewer could jump from scene to scene, close-up to close-up, and the shots would feel part of a structured whole. The cuts would feel solid, intended.

Time is nudged in the shooting with little tricks. A car may be already running when the driver climbs in so he can mime turning the ignition and take off that much faster (the editors merely cut out the premature engine noise); telephone calls go through perhaps a third faster. But it is in the editing that every moment has to truly earn its way. A pan shot, for instance, where the camera simply moves from one point of interest to another, will almost surely end up on the floor. The pan has to serve its own function—the dead space in the center may be filled with information (if we are moving over a collection of photographs, say) or it may be a source of tension (if we are waiting to see who else is in the room), but the whole move has to do something or the middle will be cut out and the pan will end up as two static shots.

In *Rope* Hitchcock tested these conventions. The film occurs entirely in real time and as a single shot (there are carefully planned invisible cuts every ten minutes when the camera runs out of film). It is a fascinating failure. Somehow our inner clock is moving faster than the film's. Despite a clever script, good, well-paced acting, and brilliant use of the camera, the film has a curiously flaccid quality. It cries out for tightening.

In Hollywood movies we never see a door open or close if the editors can help it. Not all the way. Most entrances aren't really entrances; the actor, the car, the plane is already partway on-screen when the cut occurs. Most exits leave a piece of the person in the frame. Edits have to uphold the integrity of the movie space—people can't feel like they're popping from place to place—but nonetheless, if offscreen actions were allowed to take their full time (unlocking and opening a door, for example, or walking up a driveway from a car to a house) they would seem unrealistically, excruciatingly long. So the editor shortens them until they feel right.

As the editing continues and the whole film tightens, many scenes that felt right in the slower rhythms of the earlier cut can be further compressed. Editors commonly look at a film and say, "I could take ten minutes out and you wouldn't even know it was gone." Oddly enough, they often can, and if they can, the new version will feel the same but better. It is expected that the editor will see more fat than the director; often only after a preview, when the director sees how the movie plays for an audience, is the editor given permission to squeeze out that final ten or fifteen minutes of film.

STORY TIME

Compression doesn't just grease the viewers' skids, it enlists them as collaborators. When you are making a film it is easy to forget that the audience is working too, drawing conclusions and projecting expectations. One of the principal pleasures for audiences is guessing what will happen next, and a well-paced movie prods them along but doesn't let them get too far ahead. When an audience trusts enough to guess but knows it will be wrong, it's hooked. The movie works.

Audiences want their overall expectations fulfilled—they want the hero to triumph and the lovers to be united—but moment to moment they want to be wrong. The voyeur in us wants to be surprised. We want the filmmaker to be cleverer than we are. For the writer, that means constantly creating expectations that (for the right kind of reasons) aren't quite fulfilled; for the editor, it means varying the rhythms of editing. Any film that becomes too metronomic becomes hard to pay attention to; a regular pace lulls even if the pace is a frantic one (Spielberg's hectic 1941 comes to mind).

The quickest way to deaden the audience impulse to join in is to tell too much, and it is remarkable how little can be too much. Good as film is at conveying emotion, it is in fact a poor way to convey information, whether that information is historical chronology or the plan for a heist. The viewer can't stop the film or slow it down to absorb it at his or her own speed, and in any case words are discounted; the audience trusts its eyes. Exposition that is crystal clear on the page baffles on-screen; worse, understanding exposition seems to be the area where audiences vary most. The only thing more confusing than saying too little is saying too much.

Inevitably, scripts have more dialogue than the film will require, but it takes a fine eye to look at a page of script and know what will be superfluous on-screen. Not only is more explanation required on the page to clarify unspoken emotions and actions, but the script has to be understood by actors and actresses, technicians and studio executives, who might not be the best judges of what the screen will add. When I rewrote *Dream Lover* for Alan Pakula, for instance, he urged me to keep in exposition lines that he knew would come out after rehearsal because he wanted the actors to have them as guides. Then, when it came time to edit the film, even more lines were cut. What seemed essential on the page performance made superfluous.

What distinguishes screenwriting from other forms of fiction is this compelling need for compactness, for concision. The great movie line says volumes in syllables: "Make my day"; "Rosebud"; "Here's looking at you, kid." There is much talk about "thinking visually," and that is commendable, but much of the advantage of visual storytelling is that it compresses so effectively. Director Alexander Mackendrick likes to tell the cautionary tale of Irving Thalberg working with an East Coast playwright on a seven-page dialogue scene designed to show a marriage gone stale. The writer wrestled it down to four pages, he says, and then got stuck, so Thalberg called in an old-time writer from the silent days. The old-timer's solution: the couple get on an elevator, and the husband doesn't bother to remove his hat (men wore hats in those days). At the next floor a pretty woman gets on. The husband hurriedly doffs his hat; his wife gives him a dirty look.

The movie writer's job is the opposite of the playwright's. The playwright's characters say more and are more articulate than their real counterparts; in order to explore in depth a crisis in the characters' lives the playwright stretches it with rubber bands of dialogue. The Hollywood movie writer, fighting time, pushing pace, constantly compresses reality into the telling moment.

The movie writer must walk a very fine line. Unlike life, in which we spend most of the time repeating ourselves to make sure we are understood, in a screenplay each dialogue exchange must advance the emotional flow of the scene. The roller-coaster passions of a twenty-minute argument, say, compress into two or three minutes. The writer's job in this regard is not much different from the editor's work of time compression—both have to make scenes feel real while they move things faster than real life.

This requires not only a sense of actual reality but an instinct for what audiences have come to accept as real. Screenwriters have some rules of thumb of their own: "If you can take out the scene and the story still works, take it out." "Always come into a scene as late in the action as possible, get out as soon as possible." "You can throw out the opening line of dialogue in almost any scene." "The average scene is three pages long. Have a damn good reason to write a longer one."

At its best, compression creates a compelling density. Every moment, every story beat does double duty or more. Paying off one expectation creates a new surprise. The characters fall in love as they dispose of the body; the young man gets revenge, but it hardens his soul. This is why screenwriters hold so fervently to their first rule: screenwriting is structure. If they can only sculpt that dense, compelling plot, any playwright can come along and, in old-timers' parlance, "Dialogue it in."

There is much talk in Hollywood about the three-act structure of scripts. People are always beefing up the second act or cleaning up the third. Syd Field in his popular handbook *Screenplay* has made a science of this, maintaining that the first act invariably breaks twenty-five or thirty minutes into a movie and the second act twenty-five or thirty before the end, by which he means events transpire at those times that radically change the course of the action. There is no doubt rough truth in this, though you could also say that no ten minutes should go by anywhere in the film without an event that radically changes the course of the action. Every story, in any medium, has to have a beginning, a middle, and an end. (It is interesting to note that Claude Berri's *Jean de Florette* has a devastating impact because it appears to violate this rule—it ends with Jean's abrupt death in midplot in what feels like a crushing second-act twist. But then the whole film is designed as the first half of a single two-part experience, continued in the second film, *Manon of the Spring*.)

Of course, avant-garde films conceived not as stories but as visual experiments obey no such constraints (though we are so imbued with the idea of a beginning, middle, and end, not only from storytelling but from music, that we look for it even there), while other films, such as Jean-Luc Godard's, are designed to frustrate our expectations and make us conscious of the conventions of the medium, along the lines of the modernist literature of Thomas Pynchon and William Gass. But Hollywood films have to reach too many people to take these liberties. As in creating space, so in creating story the Hollywood film relies on the expectations of the audience, letting the comforting shape of the experience provide a framework for the filmmaker's innovations. Even Robert Altman and Joan Tewkesbury's *Nashville*, hailed by critics as a revolutionary form of storytelling because it threaded many seemingly isolated tales in and out of each other, was no more than five conventionally shaped stories intertwined.

Ben Hecht's script for Hitchcock's *Notorious* is a superb example of classic movie construction. You might say the film is really three films at once—it is a love story between Cary Grant and Ingrid Bergman, a spy film about wresting secrets from the Nazis, and a suspense thriller about a woman in jeopardy. The story is brilliantly woven so all three threads have parallel intertwining arcs and scenes do double or triple duty—a scene where Grant seduces Bergman is also where he recruits her as a spy; later, in order to get inside information he must overcome his own jealousy and order her to marry another man. Much of the film's pleasure comes from the competing concerns ricocheting off each other in our heads— Will Ingrid Bergman crack the Nazi secret and live to tell the tale? Will Cary Grant overcome his jealousy to save her from Nazi poison?—but at bottom the film is a Hitchcock thriller and the line of jeopardy, of suspense, provides its basic underpinnings. The love story may be the soul of the picture, but its twists mirror the turns of the suspense plot.

An act change is more than a change of direction in the action. It changes the basic question the audience is asking itself. In the first act of *Notorious* we wonder whether playgirl Bergman will accept her call to duty and successfully infiltrate the gang of spies; the question is answered when Claude Rains accepts her into the Nazi nest. (In the love story, the first act question is whether Grant and Bergman will fall in love; no sooner is it answered than Grant must send his love to sleep with another man.)

Now Bergman is launched into the dangerous world of the double agent, and in the second act we are watching tensely for the Nazis to discover her duplicity. (In the love story, we're watching for Grant and Bergman to overcome their disappointment with each other for sacrificing love for duty—finally Grant cannot stand it anymore and asks to be transferred.)

When the Nazis discover Bergman, the third act begins—they decide to do away with her, and now we are hoping against hope they don't succeed. (Grant, finally convinced of Bergman's virtue, goes to save her.) Each act takes about a third of the film; each succeeding "act break" poses a new problem that ups the stakes and ratchets the tension in the theater.

Two of Hitchcock and Hecht's best scenes mark the turning points in the story. Both take place on the same set, the bedroom of Claude Rains' mother, and neither involves the stars of the film—the first occurs when Rains tells his mother he is planning to marry Bergman and the second when Rains must admit to her that his new wife is a traitor. But the brilliance of these scenes isn't that they are turning points in the movie. They are that, and more. They mark the act breaks for Bergman's story, but they are mini-acts on their own in the story of a struggle between a dominated son and his domineering mother and are so well drawn that even though mother and son are Nazi villains we hang on the outcome.

OPPOSITE PAGE
Two pivotal scenes from
Notorious

In the first scene we see Rains—for the first time in his life, we're sure—daring to assert himself against his mother's wishes. Out of sheer jealousy she warns him not to take in Bergman, but he musters up the guts to ignore her. In the second scene his mother's fears are realized. Triumphant, she orders Bergman's poisoning; humiliated, he agrees. We know now that Rains' struggle to tear himself from his mother's grasp is over, and he has lost. Even as the scene opens a new act in Bergman's story, it is the final act in the story of Rains' failed attempt to be his own man. That is the density of movie writing.

Movie structure is just that, a construct, a hierarchy of units from story beat to scene to sequence to act, each with a beginning, a middle, and an end. Not only do scenes do double duty, but a given moment may end a scene that is in the middle of a sequence beginning a new act of the story so that moment is really part of an end, a middle, and a beginning all at once. If a moment can be too comfortably labeled, chances are it isn't doing enough.

In the words of writer-director James L. Brooks, "Beginnings and endings are easy, it's the middles that are hard." "Beginning" and "end" have an inherent direction, a sense of movement built in; "middle" has the awful implication of a static weight, an obese gut hanging over the center of the story. The best way to write middles

The opening of *Roxanne*

is not to think of them as such but as interlocking beginnings and endings—things can't just coast along or the audience will leap ahead and get bored waiting for the movie to catch up. Structure is movement.

There is a critical period when a movie begins, the first five or ten minutes, when audiences haven't yet labeled it. They have suspended judgment while they decide what they are dealing with. This is a crucial time for a filmmaker, for here he or she must define the expectations the viewers will carry throughout the film. Here the audience takes its cues for pace, for tone, for what to accept as "real." Consequently, screenplays often have an introductory scene to let the audience know what it's in for, as in *Citizen Kane*, when a newsreel poses the enigma of Kane and an editor sends his reporter out in quest of Rosebud. Steve Martin maintains that a comedy must in this crucial period show off its most outrageous side or the audience won't buy it later on. (In *Roxanne*, for instance, his script opens with an otherwise superfluous duel with tennis rackets, a scene which is broader comedy than anything else in the film.)

Beyond defining expectations, there are two schools of thought about the movie opening. The high-voltage "grab 'em by the throat" approach opens a picture with an eye-popper, a promise of thrills galore. The spectacular stunts at the opening of each James Bond film are a prime example (Bond films have become as structurally stylized as Kabuki by now). The more remote approach (seen in a film like Henri-Georges Clouzot's suspense masterpiece *Le Salaire de la Peur*, or *The Wages of Fear*) holds that an audience will put up with anything for the first five or ten minutes and that the opening is an opportunity to lay groundwork for the rest of the film.

Rosemary's Baby

Hollywood studios, never comfortable sneaking up on an audience, generally prefer to sock it to 'em. They are not exactly given to trusting their material. But the high-voltage approach is potentially disappointing because it often creates expectations the movie can't meet. I know I can leave a Bond film after the opening credits because I've already seen the best part. When William Friedkin remade *Le Salaire de la Peur* as *Sorcerer* for Warner Brothers, he tacked onto the front a series of action sequences which made perfectly good story sense but set the wrong standard for the rest of the film. The fast-paced opening defined what should have been a suspense film as an action movie; when the film found its true pace, it never recovered from the false expectations.

Roman Polanski, a man with all the confidence in his material that studio executives lack, is a master of the low-key opening. *Rosemary's Baby* and *The Tenant* creep up on the viewer, and their terror is all the more chilling for it. In these films, the ad campaign is effectively the opening of the movie. It sets the tone and creates the expectations so Polanski can afford to take his time and build to his thrills. How many people walked into *Rosemary's Baby* without knowing what they were in for?

Changing tone in the middle of a movie is very risky because audiences that find their expectations thwarted can feel cheated and turn on a film. *Something Wild*, for instance, Jonathan Demme's clever and well-directed but not very popular movie, shifts in the third act from being a sexy romantic comedy to a grim battle for survival; no matter how well realized along the way, or how satisfying the ending in its own right, finally the finale risks leaving the audience unfulfilled. The rules have been changed in midstream; it is the right ending for the wrong movie. Countless comedies stumble because they move in the other direction—they define themselves as realistic comedy and rise to farce.

Even Hitchcock's *Psycho*, the film classic that shifts gears in the middle (still, perhaps, the only Hollywood film where the protagonist dies halfway through), maintains a consistent moral tone and level of realism. Janet Leigh's squalid romance and embezzlement are ideal first-act setups to psychopathic sex murder; the mad Norman Bates has nothing supernatural about him. The only movie I can think of that survives a major shift in tone is Preston Sturges' *Sullivan's Travels*, which, like *Something Wild*, begins as a comedy and becomes very grim indeed. But the film doesn't stay that way; the story resolves in a comic twist, when Sullivan confesses to his own murder, and the film ends as it began, on a light, comedic note that fulfills the expectations set up in the opening reels.

OPPOSITE PAGE
Something Wild

In this regard, what makes a good movie and what makes a satisfying movie sometimes conflict. *Fatal Attraction*, every man's worst nightmare of the wages of a bit of sin on the side, was originally made with an ending which inexorably followed out the logic of the story. In that version, Glenn Close's frizzy monstress commits suicide, framing poor Michael Douglas for her death. (The film still contains a large and dramatic close-up of Douglas putting down a carving knife, which only makes sense if you consider that his fingerprints are a vital story point in the deleted trial scene.) In the original, Douglas is convicted and our worst fears are realized —one small dalliance *can* ruin your life. When you think about it, the movie has to end that way—that's what it has been building to all along. On the other hand, watching the movie you know it damn well better not. You don't sit through an hour and a half of Glenn Close tormenting poor Michael Douglas only to watch him packed off to prison. A masterpiece of cinema art might pull it off, but this film isn't that, it's a genre piece. The style and the structure hold the implicit promise that Douglas will get his own back; we sit through the middle relishing the thought of his final revenge. The picture as released ends in a battle between Douglas and his knife-wielding nemesis in which we not only have the pleasure of watching him drown Close in a bathtub but we then watch Anne Archer, his long-suffering wife, finish her off with a forty-five. Changing the ending no doubt made *Fatal Attraction* not as good—not as

close to a masterpiece—but it certainly made it a more satisfying experience. The new ending may not have been as good, but it was better. (In Japan, where suicide has ritual connotations and tragic endings are more expected, the film was released with the original ending.)

Here the studio executive can be uniquely helpful. The director and the producer may get caught up in their art, but studio executives are implacably committed to their audience. Whatever the filmmakers might have thought, there was no way the studio was going to let *Fatal Attraction* out with an ending that so clearly flouted audience wishes. And here the executives' instincts made the movie work.

Those instincts can be misplaced, of course. Studio executives, in their fear of not giving the audience enough, put great emphasis on "big scene" endings. Crowd pleasers are full of them, from the Bond series to *Star Wars* to the Indiana Jones series or *Who Framed Roger Rabbit* or any Spielberg-godfathered entertainment such as *Young Sherlock Holmes*. But the truth is that these big endings often give the audience not more, but less. Many of these movies succeed with an audience, I'm convinced, not because of their endings but in spite of them. Bond endings in particular, which trade the wit and daredevil stunts of Bond openings for scores of extras waving assault rifles and cavernous sets collapsing, I find almost unwatchable. The movie is over before the ending begins.

The trick to ending these entertainments well, as it is in other films, is to pull out the emotional core of the film and feel it melt

Aliens

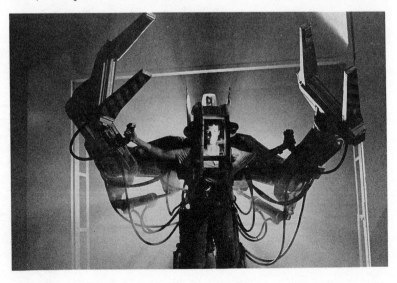

down. The *Star Wars* ending satisfies because once all the fighting is out of the way, Luke Skywalker uses The Force to pop the Death Star. *Aliens* has many big battles, humans pitted against legions of disgusting monsters; its final scene, wisely, wasn't a topper but a one-on-one battle, small by the scale of the rest of the movie. Sigourney Weaver clanks up on the evil alien queen in an exoskeleton of her very own, hissing "Come on, bitch," and we settle back for the final showdown, their bitch *mano a mano* with our bitch. The climax doesn't have to be the punchiest scene in the movie, or the cleverest; it needs to fulfill the expectations created by the rest of the film. And, of course, to surprise us even as it gives us what we're waiting for.

I seem to have strayed a long way from the simple concerns of credibility, of creating a time and place where things happen we can believe in. But have I? I have tried to describe how filmmakers serve a certain cast of mind, a way of thinking we fall into when we watch a movie. The voyeur in us is logical to a fault, impatient, picky, literal, but if properly respected it gives the special pleasures of the new and the clever, of a fresh place or a crisply thought-out story.

The voyeur, of course, is more dominant in some people than in others. It is a measure of the breadth of the film experience that these voyeuristic responses are only a part of the satisfactions of watching a movie and for most of us not the most important part at that. Some relish the complex plot of a mystery which others find needlessly confusing; some are entranced by the exotic while others are merely bored.

One of the functions movies serve is to help us define ourselves to our friends and them to us. Your friend says, "I saw *The Last Emperor.*" "Oh," you say, "what did you think," hoping, if you liked it, he did too. If he did you relax, secure in your judgment and reassured that your friend sees the world the way you do. If he didn't, you suffer a twinge of isolation. How many first dates have run aground in the fruitless search for films in common?

But even for someone who doesn't put great store in the voyeuristic delights, the basic requirements of the voyeur's eye must be met; it is an article of practical faith in Hollywood that pleasing the voyeur's eye is essential to making a film that works. The earthbound concerns of the voyeur are a necessary if not sufficient cause for us to pay attention.

OVERLEAF
The empty "big scene"
ending: *Moonraker*

Joy

Interest

Surprise

Sadness

Anger

Disgus

Distres

Fe

THE VICARIOUS EYE

KULESHOV'S FACE

In a famous experiment, the pioneer Russian filmmaker Lev Kuleshov intercut a shot of a Russian Buster Keaton—Mosjukine, an actor renowned for his expressive but deadpan face—into situations which trigger emotion: scenes with a crying baby, a bowl of soup, a coffin. Afterward the audience praised the actor's performance, remarking on how well he displayed paternal love, hunger, mourning. The actor hadn't expressed anything different from shot to shot —it was the identical, tantalizingly neutral look in every case—but Kuleshov proved that in context it took on appropriate meaning. The audience read into the actor what it would have felt in his place.

Kuleshov's point was that in film, editing is all: context determines meaning. But underneath, Kuleshov's experiment illustrates a yet more fundamental truth about the psychology of vision: people have an innate empathic instinct. If we see a face we have a natural, automatic impulse to divine what the person behind the face is feeling, to test that emotion inwardly to see if it is suitable and, if it is, to taste it as our own. If it's not there, as in the Russian experiment, we will even try to fill in what's missing.

As sad as any film I've ever seen is footage shot in the 1940s by Dr. René Spitz of infants in the care of the state because their mothers were in prison. Clean, diapered, lying untouched in their

OPPOSITE PAGE
Dr. Izard's eight basic expressions and Ivan Mosjukine as *Casanova*

starched cribs, their faces display a shocking maturity of grief. We have all seen more graphic violence and pain on film, but for me what made this more ghastly than grislier scenes was an overpowering sense of my helplessness—those grave figures demanded to be held, stroked, comforted, even though they were only flickering images on a screen and now, forty years later, probably parents in their own right. Their infant faces not only portray their grief; they are an implacable call for help.

Long before we can talk, we are attuned to the shifting sands of expression. The first thing a baby recognizes is a human face; we now know that a baby only weeks old has complex exchanges with his mother, telling her something by his expression, reading her expression in response. Charles Darwin theorized that some emotions are innate and universal and that they are linked to specific facial expressions which evolved as a way for the helpless infant to convey his needs. Recently, specialists in child development have proved him correct and codified an internationally recognized list of eight fundamental expressions that emerge in early childhood and send the same message from child to mother the world over.

Our response to human emotion is as automatic as the physiological responses to shapes and patterns Arnheim described in his innovative work on art and perception. Just as the human eye seeks pattern and balance in an image automatically, as a function of our physiology, so the eye instinctually searches for emotion in the human face. And we are not passive observers of those emotions. The emotions of others create a matching urge on our part—to comfort them, to protect ourselves, to respond to their smile with a smile of our own. We are wired that way.

But Kuleshov's actor was impassive. Viewers weren't reacting to his emotion, they were reading onto his blank face what they thought he should be feeling, that is, what they would have been feeling in his place. After all, unlike life the relationship with the screen is one-sided—the viewer responds to the actor, but the actor flickers along oblivious of the reaction. So the viewer must supply his own explanations for the actor's behavior. The viewer performs a dual role, empathy, yes, but something more, he projects his own feelings into the characters. And it seems the special power of film, of those enormous faces twenty feet high, lit for meaning, to open channels of vicarious experience untapped by books or theater.

The vicarious eye sees with the heart. It mixes our yearning to matter—to be taken seriously, to have our emotions count—with our need to please others, to read the slightest shift in their feelings and accommodate to it. The vicarious eye puts our heart in the actor's body: we feel what the actor feels, but we judge it for ourselves. Unlike relationships in life, here we can give ourselves up to other people in full confidence that we will always be in command. If they let us down, if they cheat our sense of what they should be feeling, we can turn on them, even mock them gleefully, without the slightest fear of reprisal.

Nonetheless, there is more at stake in the vicarious transaction than the voyeuristic one. We have invested part of ourselves in another person, or at least in the image of another person; if that person fulfills his promise, he can transport us into a world of intensely felt emotion. The voyeuristic experience may be grand or clever, but the vicarious experience can be profoundly moving.

The vicarious experience is not bound by iron bands of logic but by silken cords of emotional truth. Human response is so layered, so nuanced, so elastic that almost any action can seem reasonable if we are shown the emotional substrate on which it rests. When my son was six years old, he and I waited for weeks for him to lose his first tooth; when it finally came out, I shouted with pride and excitement, rather the way I thought he would. But instead of celebrating he burst into tears. He seemed positively terrified, and I was worried and confused and a little scared myself. What had gone wrong? No, he explained, it didn't hurt, sometimes good things made him cry. (Was the idea of growing up scarier than he expected it to be?)

When I heard his explanation I felt relief, and I let the old feeling of excitement back in. My son's reaction had been illogical and completely out of character, but it was also exactly right. Living the moment through my son's eyes I gained a truer sense of its real importance and new respect for him. Such is the stuff of the vicarious experience.

On film, the combination of the intense emotions aroused and the one-way nature of the transaction creates an eerie, sometimes volatile mix. At its most extreme, when someone confuses his relation to the screen with a real relationship, a John Hinckley tries to kill a real American President to save the Jodie Foster he knows from *Taxi Driver*. But for the normal viewer, the vicarious thrill is enough—the chance to react to the character even as we are him, to give ourselves up to him while admiring (or loathing) him from the outside.

The tension between the two impulses—the urge to be the character and to judge him simultaneously—gives the vicarious experi-

Claude Rains meeting his
fate at the end of *Notorious*

ence grit. One of Hitchcock's adages was "the better the villain the better the picture." The Claude Rains character in *Notorious*, for instance, is certainly the most interesting character in the film, the most dimensional and least caricatured. We sympathize with his plight—we feel with him his humiliation before his domineering mother, his disillusionment when the woman he loves turns out to be using him—but we still loathe his Nazi guts. In the end, when he returns to certain death at the hands of his accomplices, we feel a frisson of regret and glee. Even as we hiss a more cartoonish heavy, a Darth Vader or a Goldfinger, we indulge his fantasies of omnipotent control, of self-indulgence and flagrant abuse of power, of pure ego or pure id run amok.

In the star, however, our impulse to empathy and our judgment of character don't grate, they amplify each other. We're proud to feel what stars feel. We wish we could be more like them. Yet their exemplary qualities don't explain their hold on us. They have a special power: whatever the mysterious quality we all radiate that triggers empathy, stars exude its distilled essence. They glow brighter. Like the miserable babies in Dr. Spitz's documentaries, they don't request our empathy, they demand it.

Part of their special appeal, some say, is the feeling that they are holding something back. There is some part of Robert Redford, or Paul Newman, or Jack Nicholson, or Meryl Streep (or even Madonna or Sean Penn) that the audience knows it will never know. They are admirable, desirable; you want to be them, if only for the space of a film, and yet you know you don't really know who they are.

The stars who understand their own appeal cultivate the mystery by staying out of the public eye. Talk shows showed me the real Burt Reynolds (or at least made me think so); he seemed like a charming, witty guy I might like for a friend, but the mystery, the sense of his being more intensely, grandly human than I am, melted away. When I see him on the screen he's not a star anymore, he's an actor. What would have happened to James Dean if he had been a talk-show regular?

The star's withholding quality is a lure to get to know him better, a promise that this time, this film, you will finally break through and make him your own. At the same time it implies that the star has a self-sufficiency, a completeness you will never have—you, after all, would be happy to have him get to know all about you. It gives the star a bedrock core—it makes you think he has some special strength at his center, while deep down you know that in your center there is only a hole of doubt and confusion. It makes him better than you are, in a way which arouses not animosity but awe.

The give-it-all-you've-got-type stars, like Liza Minnelli, or Sally Field, or Mickey Rooney, don't feel like stars to me, but I suppose you could argue they work so hard at inviting you in that people are flattered to be asked. They are so open, begging you so fervently to feel what they're feeling, that they do half your work. While the withholding star lures you in by daring you to understand him, the effusive star drags you in by your hair whether you want in or not. Effusive stars are less in the heroic mold than the touchingly vulnerable—we know that in their secret core is the same desperate loneliness we all feel, but we admire their mighty labors to transcend it.

What both types share is what film editors and acting teachers call "energy." This is a hard-to-define quality since even a performer as sad-sack as Buster Keaton is said to possess it, but it can transform an actor of no particular physical distinction, a Dustin Hoffman or a James Woods, into a compelling star. It is a quality of performance which projects a sense of absolute emotional reality but reality more intense than we experience in life. As Satyajit Ray

Gert Frobe and Sean Connery in *Goldfinger*

has remarked, a star is someone you can watch doing nothing. Even the most withholding stars, a Garbo, say, project a vitality of emotion which invites us to share in their inner world. It is an electric force, but it is also a peculiar sort of emotional transparency, an ability to let us look straight inside their heads and read what they are feeling. Ingrid Bergman had this quality, as did Richard Burton. And it's not surprising that it made them stars. Intense, honest emotions are a valuable commodity; they are hard to come by, and they make us feel alive. Our vicarious eye scans our environment for emotional beacons; when we find one, we lock in.

Actors and actresses search for great parts, and there is much complaining about their dearth. But what is a great part for a movie actor? It is certainly not a great character in the novelistic sense. No matter how brilliant the characterization, a movie can never probe the inner workings of the mind the way a good novel can. In film, we are constantly told, "Action is character": the compelling movie character is a man whose thoughts are read in his deeds. Nuance or ambivalence cloud the issue. They confuse the action. So Hollywood movies tend to trade in strongly delineated, driven characters, characters of few words. Actors trained in theater judge the importance of their parts by the number of lines of dialogue and are not above maneuvering to give their character more to say. In movies the opposite can be true. There is a story that Clint Eastwood once counseled Steve McQueen to give the other guy the words—the less you say, he advised, the stronger you are. Clint is a movie actor. In John Ford's words, "That's how to make 'em good actors. Don't let any of 'em talk!"

Although in movies action is character, we shouldn't fool ourselves into thinking that in real life character is action. Even the greatest of screen characters, Charles Foster Kane, for example, cannot begin to reveal the depths and complexity of a character drawn by Proust or Dostoyevski. When complex characters are portrayed on the screen, in theater adaptations like *Long Day's Journey into Night* or *Hamlet* or in novel adaptations such as *Sophie's Choice*, we tend to admire the character more than we relish the movie experience. Profound characters don't make great movies. That is a prime reason a pulp novel is at least as likely as a great novel to make a good film.

What makes a great movie part? A part that somehow expresses the essence of a star. A part that fits the persona of one of those

Humphrey Bogart as Sam Spade in *The Maltese Falcon*

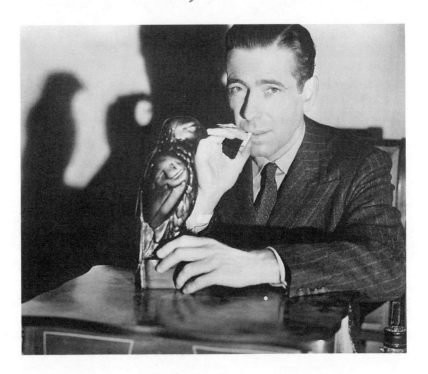

rare actors with star presence so well that it is impossible to separate the two in your mind: Clint Eastwood as the Man with No Name, Bogart as Sam Spade, William Powell and Myrna Loy as Nick and Nora Charles, Diane Keaton as Annie Hall. A great part is as much a function of great casting as great writing.

It is not hard to see, then, why making movies based on movies has proved to be such a dead end. To remake a movie is to strip-mine the material—you will only skim off the surface of what is already mostly surface. You will lose the essence of the performance, the actor, and you will build on an already attenuated version of human behavior.

Casting a star in a dark role stands the vicarious world on its head. The very qualities that draw us in are twisted into something we despise: Bogart's grating obsessiveness, the essence of Sam Spade, is also what leads his character to betray his partners in *The Treasure of the Sierra Madre*; the quiet, resolute integrity of Henry Fonda in *Young Mr. Lincoln* and *The Grapes of Wrath* becomes the tight-lipped, resolute evil of a man who will shoot a defenseless child in *Once Upon a Time in the West*. If a film is only as good as its heavy, these are the best films of all.

Henry Fonda in *The Grapes of Wrath* and *Once Upon a Time in the West*

THE MOMENT

I was an earnest documentary filmmaker when Alan Pakula gave me my first break in features as the American Film Institute intern on *The Parallax View*. My first job was every young man's fantasy of Hollywood: I was paid a hundred dollars a week, given an office and a desk, and told to audition actresses for the role of a sixteen-year-old nymphomaniac. I placed an ad in the trades, talked to agents (God knows what they thought of me), and saw a trickle of young hopefuls, mostly blond baton twirlers from the San Fernando Valley, who sat on the other side of my desk, read the pages I gave them, and tried very hard to please, which as you can imagine was the best part. Occasionally, a truly talented actress whose agent didn't know better came through the office, but most of the real prospects had more direct ways to attract the attention of the director, which was just as well because I knew nothing about acting and wouldn't have known what to say to a really good actress anyway.

Eventually, I got called into the director's office. An old friend had put him onto a hot prospect, an attractive young lady sitting demurely in the chair across from *his* desk. Pakula wanted to read her. Warren wasn't around, would I please read his part?

It was a dumb scene, a sort of male fantasy of the compliant, voracious sexual groupie bedeviling poor old Warren Beatty. No sooner had we started to read than the actress announced this wasn't any good, she had to act it out, would that be all right? Pakula said fine, whatever makes you comfortable, so she said okay, that's the door, this is my suitcase, and she got to work.

I was honored with one of the supreme erotic experiences of my life. This beautiful woman turned, looked at me, and suddenly I was indeed the man of her dreams. I suddenly knew the scene we were playing was only a ruse, an excuse for her to tell me what was really on her mind: that she wanted me more than anything she had ever wanted in her life. She teased me, she begged me, toward the end she even started unbuttoning my shirt, as I struggled to read Warren's lines through eyeballs swollen with blood.

Then, as suddenly as it began, it was over. While I took a few stabs at buttoning my shirt, wondering how anyone could hear over the pounding of my heart, the actress and Pakula discussed her reading. Would he like it with a Southern accent? Was she trying to play sixteen or eighteen? Would braces make her look younger? After she left, and I had recovered enough to form a sentence, he asked me if she wasn't too old.

She was too old. She never got the part, which ended up on the floor anyway. Had I known then what I know now about screen time it would have been obvious that it wasn't the sort of scene that would earn its way, and I suspect the director already knew as much, that the scene was in the script for political reasons, that the reading was an act of politeness to the actress and his friend, and that my assignment and my part in the reading were a sort of wonderful welcoming present to the big time. But in the process Pakula had also given me something more, a supreme introduction to the glories of truly gifted performance. I had watched a beautiful woman fall deeply in love with me for five minutes.

For the voyeuristic eye, credibility depends on plausibility: "that couldn't happen" is a damning indictment. For the vicarious eye, however, credibility depends on emotional truth: the criticism is not "that couldn't happen" but "he wouldn't do that." A critical part of the empathic process, it seems, is a testing stage. We watch, lured by the emotional beacon; we test the feelings against our sense of emotional truth; if we are not convinced, we laugh, ignore the outburst, or even feel insulted by the swindle, but if we are won over we give ourselves up to the shared experience no matter how implausible it is. This process has its roots, no doubt, in our earliest exchanges, when as infants our survival depended on reading the true feelings of the powerful adults who controlled our lives; it bears fruit in the awesome persuasive power of emotional truth. That actress had the astonishing gift of truth, and I had no choice but to respond. Even though she was sitting in the director's office reading from a script I was absolutely convinced she loved me.

Clearly, there are degrees. Scottie telling Captain Kirk "She canna take the strain" does it well enough for me to think the starship *Enterprise* is in danger, if I'm so disposed, but he's not fooling anybody. Skilled acting can simulate emotion, and that is usually enough. But in the editing a clear division emerges between the actor who supplies a competent, even able performance and the one who projects real truth. Often in the dailies it is hard to tell, but when, as the film is shaped, the scene is run hundreds of times, a higher standard of performance emerges.

After twenty or thirty runnings most actors' work begins to show. It is only natural that as the freshness of the experience wears off we watch with a more jaded eye. But what are we seeing we didn't see the first five or ten times? It is hard to say why exactly, but the emotions start to feel applied rather than evoked. The actor and the part delaminate. This is true of almost all performances, even well-respected ones. I doubt John Houseman's job in *The Paper Chase* would stand this scrutiny, though it won him an Oscar and served the picture well.

On rare occasions a performance feels just as real on the hundredth viewing. I wager almost any performance by Spencer Tracy will. Jane Fonda is capable of this; so are Gene Hackman and Dustin Hoffman. This uncanny ability to project bedrock truth is a quality of the performer, not the part, a tenacious, even self-destructive gut need for honesty. It cannot be taught. It is the quintessence of movie acting.

A good director doesn't need to see the performance a hundred times to catch the difference. He or she can assess an actor's strengths and use them for what truth they can project. Houseman in *The Paper Chase* is a case in point. As an actor, his entire range lies between supercilious irk and high dudgeon; in this film the director, James Bridges, and his editor, Walter Thompson, shaped his performance carefully, limiting him narrowly to moments of ire. To judge from the final result, where Houseman had to express something else they showed as little of him as possible and relied on Kuleshov's trick of the impassive face, betting that Houseman's curmudgeonly scenes were good enough that we would fill in his emotions for the rest if they kept the rest to a bare minimum.

The director creates an emotional climate to nurture empathy. Editors can save a performance, good actors can direct themselves, but only the director can give a film the gift of life. In Hollywood the idea of auteur cinema is a standing joke, but the fact remains that a good film portrays a consistent view of what makes people tick, and that view is the director's. People talk of "pace," and "tone" and "mood," and "the directorial sensibility," but what a film reveals, if the director is in command of the medium, is the director's sense of emotional truth. The director is the one who decides, "Yes, that will do, that feels right to me," and unless the director abdicates responsibility, or loses control of the actors and the material (something it is all too easy to do), the movie will reflect those decisions. This is the strength of John Ford, François Truffaut, Miloš Forman, the best of Altman; when a film like *Bull Durham* comes along by a new director (Ron Shelton in this case), we can instantly tell that he is a real movie director, not a traffic cop, because he infuses his film with life. He makes it feel ample, large-spirited; the emotional flow isn't forced to fit the procrustean bed of story, and it doesn't feel manipulative. It feels like life, if not our life, then life on a nearby planet.

For the voyeuristic eye, the relentless march of the plot paces the picture. Time is hastened along from story beat to story beat. But the vicarious eye isn't watching plot points, it's searching for real emotion. For the vicarious eye the basic unit isn't the story beat but the actor's moment, that single pure note of emotional truth when the actor's pitch is perfect and his intensity is high. The moments are the pearls of performance the director watches for on the set and the editor treasures during cutting.

Good moments are strewn through any good film, but great moments, perfect pitch at the crucial turning points, are its emotional heart. Think of a movie, and if you aren't thinking of an epic spectacle or a dash of action chances are you are thinking of a great moment: Paul Newman, the pool hustler, cradling his shattered hands and sobbing to Piper Laurie, "They broke my thumbs"; Marlon Brando, in a voice cracked with hopeless yearning, asserting, "I coulda been a contender"; the murderous Al Pacino as the new Godfather falsely swearing to Diane Keaton that he didn't kill his brother-in-law; Meryl Streep's soul tearing in half as she makes Sophie's choice.

These are the money shots of the empathic world, and producers and directors know they deserve extra expense and effort to get right. However, while the trouble and expense of the voyeuristic money shot—the epic master—is right there on the screen, here the producer's money buys an invisible asset, time, a chance for actor and director to linger over the scene, to do it again and again until it really works.

Directors love moments. Given the director's inexorable task— how to make each scene work, all by itself, day after day on the set —moments are gold. If you are under the spell of a moment, the director doesn't have to surprise you or tease you or titillate you, or worry if it's fast enough or what it brings to the story. In a moment, story time stands still. Moments make great dailies and unforgettable high points in any film. In editing any scene the editor tries to moor it to its own, smaller moments.

But while these atoms of emotional truth give the scene credibility and bite, from the editor's standpoint they have one crucial

OVERLEAF
The moment: Rod Steiger and Marlon Brando in *On the Waterfront*

quality which makes them antithetical to the story beat—in a moment, time stands still. The rush of plot is suspended while we savor the empathic pleasures of the moment. This is all to the good in the peak scenes of the film—in fact, one could argue that the purpose of the plot is to allow such unforgettable moments to exist in the first place. When Sophie makes her choice or Marlon Brando pours out his heart to Rod Steiger in the back of a limousine we want it to take as long as it takes. We're not thinking about where it will lead us—we are where we are trying to go.

Yet if a director is too seduced by emotional impact for its own sake, if every scene is directed for its maximum dose of vicarious truth, the timeless pauses slow the story until the film grinds to a halt, mired in moments. The voyeur in us stops watching. There are all too many forgettable films with great moments (*True Confessions*, with Robert De Niro and Robert Duvall, comes to mind). Though Hitchcock caught some dillies of moments, such as the famous thirty-second kiss in *Notorious*, his films are remembered more for sequences, like the shower sequence in *Psycho* or the wine-cellar-key sequence in *Notorious*. Even Alan Pakula, a connoisseur of the moment as a producer and a master of the moment as a director, says that the more he works, the less important moments are to him in shaping a movie. The job of editing is a balancing act between the rhythmic demands of the vicarious and the voyeuristic, a search for the center of gravity of that particular experience.

Like sculpting in clay, film editing is a process of adding on and paring away, but unlike the sculptor the editor begins with a fixed number of choices, the different shots which make up the coverage of the scene. A good director, of course, doesn't just present the editor with a menu of shots but has a specific pattern in mind which tells the story and captures its emotional rhythms best. Most plan out their pattern with little drawings before they shoot.

Some, like Hitchcock, claim to shoot only exactly what they need and imply that editing is a mechanical process, film's version of painting by numbers. Some, like George Stevens, rely on a great range of coverage, giving themselves the widest breadth of options in the cutting. But most lie in between, lacking the nerve or the budget of a George Stevens and the specific genius of a Hitchcock which allowed him to visualize his scenes so precisely in advance.

Even Hitchcock, legendary in this regard, might have been indulging in a bit of self-promotion. In *Hitchcock* by François Truffaut he boasts that for the shower sequence in *Psycho* he shot seventy camera setups for forty-five seconds of finished footage. The finished scene is a masterpiece, but it doesn't have anywhere near seventy setups. Using slow-motion video we can count them: the entire three-minute bathroom scene has only forty-five setups, and the forty-five seconds in question have twenty-two (though some are used more than once). What happened to the other twenty-five (or forty-eight) setups? Perhaps even Hitchcock shot coverage and shaped his film in the editing room.

When directors shot three movies a year they had to leave most of the editing in other hands. John Ford, for instance, was often away shooting another picture while his films were being put together. Episodic television is still made this way, but today no self-respecting director would abdicate the editing room of a feature film. For at least four months after shooting ends, and often much longer, the director is at the editor's beck and call; while the editor may spend a few hours or even days assembling something alone, the director is there at the editor's side when the final decisions are made.

Unlike shooting, editing is a trial-and-error process. The editor tries different takes and different camera angles until the scene feels right, then shows it to the director (unless the director is there all the time); if the director doesn't like what the editor has done, they can pull it apart and try something else. This gives the director an absolute control impossible during shooting, when decisions must be quick and final; paradoxically, this can make directors more open to suggestion because they have the freedom to change their mind. Exactly what the editor or the director contribute varies with each relationship, but it is no accident that the best directors search out exceptional editors. As Pakula says, he wants their "magic fingers."

Editors usually have to start work while the director is still shooting so except for notes in dailies or the occasional Saturday meeting they make the first cut on their own. Keeping in mind the director's dicta and the requirements of orientation and story—making spatial relationships clear, keeping the plot moving—the editor turns him- or herself over to the material, trying to sense the emotional line of the scene. The editor asks, "Who do we want to be on?" by which the editor means who is the emotional center of the scene at that moment—whose emotional beacon lures most strongly—and cuts the scene accordingly. Formulaic TV editing automatically shows us the person talking, but often we want to be on someone else, the person absorbing the talk or waiting to butt in. A good editor cuts for feeling.

Once the editor assembles the scene with roughly the right shots in the right order, he or she screens the work and refines. Usually, there is no obvious solution, no matter what the director intended, because the editor must decide between conflicting demands for screen coverage; the editor might want to jump from one close-up to another to show a brief reaction or interjection, for instance, but the beat might be too short and disorient the viewer or break the rhythms of the scene, or an actor's performance might be so irredeemably bad the editor cannot show it even though that is where we want to be.

First cuts, which include every beat of the story, almost always come in too long. Filmmakers usually walk out of dailies buoyed up; they leave first cuts weighted down. What they envisaged as deft or deeply moving feels sodden and deadly dull, the emotional impact buried under repetition and a dogged determination to tell more than anyone wants to know.

Consequently, the editor cultivates a finely tuned impatience. Once the first cut is in place the editor and the director pore over the scenes, asking themselves if each beat, each moment earns its way. Like anything else, a movie gets better if the weakest parts are cut away, but even if parts aren't weak but irrelevant they hurt the film too. Irrelevancies have a deadening cumulative effect—it is another rule of thumb, remember, that if two scenes feel the same the shorter one is better.

But tightening and improving are only superficially what editing is about. Editors are generally talented and experienced men and women and could on their own fashion a tight, well-paced first cut of a film without much guidance from the director. But most directors won't let them. The encyclopedic first assembly is a depressing but necessary step; this is the block of granite from which the movie is hewn. For while the work is like a sculptor's when he molds clay, adding and subtracting, the mind-set is like a sculptor's when he chisels granite—the editor is confronted with a block of marble, the footage, and has to take away everything that isn't the film. Somewhere in that mass of dailies is the movie. Only when it is all together, when the scenes are made to work one by one, does the essence of the film emerge.

If the director and the actor have done their job on the set, the actor's performance is designed with as much of a beginning, middle, and end as the story—often, it is the shape of the performance which gives the story its punch. Think of the shy young romantic who becomes the embittered spinster in *The Heiress*, the wimpy pushover who becomes the avenging terror in *Straw Dogs*, the idealistic GI who becomes the remorseless Mafia don in *The Godfather*. But over weeks of shooting, often out of sequence, it is nigh impossible to calibrate each scene perfectly on the set. Many directors try to give themselves leeway, particularly in crucial scenes, and shoot versions at varying emotional pitch so they can tune the film in the editing.

The character arc: Katharine Hepburn in *The African Queen:* before and (with Humphrey Bogart) after.

They might discover that what looked emotionally powerful in the dailies becomes absurd when it is strung together. We judge emotional truth partly by context. On the simplest level, it is a matter of tone, how one character measures against the others—a character from *Roxanne* would be ridiculous in *Taxi Driver*, for instance—but we also test the character against itself. A woman breaks down in one scene, and we are moved. A woman breaks down in every scene, and it's a running gag. Her consistent overwrought intensity makes us distrust her emotions, no matter how affectingly portrayed. How many times can a character cry in a movie, how many times can she be furious, before it becomes a joke?

Selecting which moments to jettison is deciding the shape of the actor's performance and the emotional arc of the film. The editor and director might discover, for instance, that a scene they thought was about a man's anger at his wife for walking out on him was really about her pain at leaving, that what they played for counterpoint should be the main theme for the scene to work. The change in that scene might lead them to work through the whole film to throw more emphasis on the woman's suffering.

While the editor's voyeuristic eye is pushing and trimming, hurrying along the story, the editor's vicarious eye cannot be rushed. You cannot hurry a moment. Unlike the story beat, which begs for compression, the moment is an irreducible kernel of emotional truth. An editor cutting a love scene shot in close-ups, for example, moves back and forth between the two faces of the lovers, sensing the emotional flow of the scene and reflecting it in the cutting. The editor will try to give the scene more impact by compressing it—by cutting out unnecessary beats, redundant pauses, the weakest moments. But cutting into a true acting moment can only diminish it. If the editor trims the beginning or the end it will feel truncated, mechanical; if the editor cuts away in the middle to the shot of the other lover in order to compress the performance (by showing five seconds of the lover, for instance, and deleting twenty-five seconds of the original shot) the act of cutting away itself guts the intensity of the performance. When editing an emotional scene beats can be cut out, but speeding moments along saps their emotional truth. Even a great performance suffers—in *Pelle the Conqueror*, for instance, Max von Sydow's brilliant portrayal is consistently weakened by cutting away from him in the middle of his moments.

So, like it or not, the editor is stuck with the director's sense of emotional pace. The right length for a moment is very hard to estimate on the set, and even harder to control, since the test of the moment is truth—the actor must feel it and live it. If a director tells the actor to do the same thing but faster (and some directors do) the result is often an ersatz moment, and in the editing room the longer, truer moment demands to be used.

Let us return to our scene of the woman walking out on her husband. Suppose her pain is the subject of the scene. But suppose her husband has given the director a series of brilliant, but very long, moments. Wonderful moments. If the director, lacking the intestinal fortitude to throw them out, utters the words every editor dreads, "I know, but it's too good to lose," the editor is left with two choices: either throw the scene out of whack by shifting the emphasis onto the husband, which pushes the audience off the emotional center of the film, or beef up the wife's part, extending her moments to balance out the scene, thereby giving it undue weight, slowing the film and weakening her performance. If a movie is a series of scenes where all the actors have nothing but moments too good to lose, it can end up a wonderfully acted, almost unwatchable film. *True Confessions* comes to mind. Or *The Pope of Greenwich Village*, or *Ironweed*.

Just as spectacle by itself becomes boring, and our voyeuristic mind must be stimulated by the insistent beat of the story, so the moment by itself palls and the vicarious mind must be galvanized by the urgency of discord. The emotional equivalent of turn-the-page story tension is conflict between characters, where their true nature is revealed. Conflict draws us from moment to moment by our empathic curiosity and our competitive instincts: "Is he who we think he is?" "Will she stand the strain?" "Who will prevail?" Conflict pulls us inside the characters' skin and forces us to take sides.

Think of a skillfully written lovers' quarrel—for instance, the Ingrid Bergman rendezvous with Cary Grant on the park bench late in *Notorious*, when she is dying from Nazi poison and Grant is too jealous to notice. He accuses Bergman of high living and won't take her illness seriously; she is stung by his contempt and won't reveal how sick she really is. This is Bergman's scene, and the more obtuse Grant acts the more intensely we feel her dilemma. Although we are touched by the ardor of Grant's jealousy we want to pick him up by the lapels and shake some sense into him. Their conflict makes us care.

If the scene were badly written or acted we would be impatient with Grant's blindness or Bergman's reticence—they would feel like phony theatrical conventions—but because we believe the characters we are on the edge of our seats, egging them on, hoping Grant finally will have enough faith in Bergman to put aside his wounded pride and trust her. Our empathy creates expectations which we project on the arguing characters; those expectations create their own suspense, as we watch to see if they will be fulfilled. And we are pulled through the scene.

When the writer creates a scene, when the director stages it, when the editor cuts it, each asks the editor's question: "Who do we want to be on?" One of the greatest pleasures of watching a well-made movie is putting ourselves in the hands of filmmakers whose empathic instincts we can trust, of giving ourselves up to their rhythms as they clearly lead us through an emotional labyrinth, switching our empathic allegiance with clear, deft strokes. (This is not the actor's concern. Generally, actors have to convince them-

Cary Grant and Ingrid Bergman on the park bench in *Notorious*

selves the scene is centered on them, and they rewrite their scenes in their minds from their own point of view. This is not simply ego, but a necessary step in taking possession of a role, though it can be taken too far—some actors when they're offered a script only read their own lines.)

Emotional pacing is as critical as story pacing and more delicate. Writer, director, and editor all have to keep the scene shifting from one character to another, not simply by alternating who has the lines but internally, so we enter the characters' inner lives and feel along with them. These empathic beats can be extremely brief—as short as a single line of dialogue or even a sideways look, but both writer and director work on the assumption that at any given instant our vicarious eye can only look into the mind of a single character.

Though our allegiance in a scene may be split, as in the love scene from *Notorious*, at any moment we can only be feeling what one of the characters feels.

We can, however, see one character through the other's eyes. Our allegiance may be split, but we are not impartial observers. It is Bergman's scene. Like most of the movie, we are seeing it from her point of view. We don't share Grant's skepticism because we know something he doesn't: she really is being poisoned. We have a rooting interest in Bergman, and when we watch Grant we feel his emotions but we are also seeing him through Bergman's eyes. We want him to believe her as much as Bergman does.

Yet we feel for Grant too. If we didn't the scene would be pure melodrama. Switching back and forth heightens the empathic power of both characters—feeling Grant's annoyance makes us feel Bergman's desperation all the more.

Think of the climactic scene in *East of Eden* when Raymond Massey confronts his favored son, Richard Davalos, the morning after the young man has been shown by his misfit brother, James Dean, that their mother is a whore. Davalos has been on a drunken tear all night; now Massey has gone to stop him from shipping out on a troop train in a final self-destructive act.

The scene starts with Massey running along the crowded platform, searching the train windows, desperately calling his son's name (the only dialogue in the scene); we feel the father's distress and his frantic desire to save his son. Then we cut to Davalos, slumped drunkenly at the window of the train. He's a shocking sight —no longer the clean-cut, self-righteous youth we've seen before but exhausted, sodden, and wild about the eyes. We leave the father's feelings behind while we feel the emptiness of the son's disillusionment; then he sights his father and lifts his head with an angry sneer. Now from the son's pain and anger we cut back to the father's shock—first at the boy's sad state, then at the contempt in his eyes (his son has never looked at him like this). We return to the son to catch his pleasure at his father's dismay. With a hysterical chuckle he drives his anger home by smashing his head through the window glass—and then we're back with the father, who recoils as if he'd been butted hard between the eyes. The father's flinch throws us back to the son—his reaction makes the son laugh, but it's a strange laugh to watch. Though the sounds coming out are laughter, the boy looks as if he's crying.

Over Massey's back we see the train start to carry the boy away just as James Dean rushes up. Massey collapses unconscious into

his second son's arms—but we don't see Massey's expression as he faints, we see Dean catch him and cradle him, showing us only enough of Massey to know he's passed out, because now the emotional baton has been passed to the second son, now his emotions are what we want to feel. We cut briefly to the dark shape of the disappearing brother, then back to a tighter shot of Dean (Massey is completely hidden now in his son's arms—this is Dean's moment, and we don't want to be distracted). Dean watches his brother vanish and we feel his pain; then, in a brilliant bit of acting, he looks down at his unconscious father, and we feel his pain transmute into guilt. In about fifty seconds, without a line of dialogue, we have been led through a complex emotional transaction—father's concern becomes son's anger becomes father's pain becomes second son's guilt.

The principle of empathic flow can serve less high-minded purposes. Writers rely on this effect, for instance, when they are stuck with writing an impossible scene and, as they say, "Hang a lantern on it," take the curse off the viewer's objections by having a character state them. As long as somebody on-screen thinks what's going on is ridiculous, as long as the audience can transfer its doubts into the mind of one of the characters, the screenwriter is off the hook. What was a viewer's inner criticism becomes one of the character's points of view. This can give the film a sort of hip in-on-the-joke quality; in tied or tired hands, the tongue-in-cheek can be a poor substitute for the hard work of making the characters and the story more credible.

OPPOSITE PAGE
One frame from every cut of the train station sequence in *East of Eden*.

Directors can use this indirect effect to lend credibility to a dangerously sentimental scene: they know that watching through the eyes of one of the characters allows the viewer to indulge feelings he otherwise might question. In *Drums Along the Mohawk*, for instance, we don't just watch proud father Henry Fonda rocking his new baby, we watch his wife watching him with adoring eyes. Her feelings cue ours and give us permission to feel shamelessly sentimental.

Subtle changes in the pace and rhythm of scenes can have enormous effect on the empathic flow. In this regard editing is much underrated by studio executives, critics, and audiences generally. A knowledgeable audience might leave the theater feeling vaguely dissatisfied or critical of the writing or the performances, when an editor will know that the film was poorly cut.

The first assembly of *All the President's Men* is an example. It had the usual rough-cut lethargy, but it had another unsettling quality—the scenes didn't register. They were literally unwatchable. The mind glided over them as they paraded by. When we examined them more closely, we discovered that the main editor, Bob Wolfe, had in fact done too good a job. The scenes were too polished. He had been trained by Sam Peckinpah (he had cut on *The Wild Bunch* and *Straw Dogs*) and had adopted Peckinpah's style of motivating his cuts by tiny dialogue overlaps so that in a scene between two people shot separately, in "singles," the last half word spoken by one person would extend into the shot of the other, or the first half word of the second would precede his appearance on-screen. These slight sound "heads and tails" have the effect of smoothing out the cuts so they aren't as noticeable, in editor's terms, "greasing the cut."

This worked fine for Peckinpah, the way he designed his scenes, but for Pakula it spelled disaster. "I want people to notice the cuts," Pakula said. "If I didn't want cuts I wouldn't have them." Singles are a common way to shoot scenes, but here Pakula had used them for a particular reason: the film was built around a series of confrontations, scenes of the reporters trying to pry information from reluctant informants. Pakula wanted the distance and the opposition that comes from having each actor in his own shot. Greasing the cuts removed the very tension that drove the scene.

Pakula and Wolfe went through the film, removing overlaps and adding empty space on the heads and tails of shots, and the film came alive. That beat of dead space brought out the uncertainty and sense of separation between the reporter and his subject, and suddenly we cared enough to pay attention. Now there was conflict. Now we were engaged with the reporters in their quest. It was one of the rare occasions when making a film longer made it feel shorter.

EMOTIONAL SPACE

While the voyeuristic eye demands scenes grounded firmly in the solid geometry of three-dimensional space, the vicarious eye makes no such requirement. Its space is the inner space where a character lives his emotional life. Sets and costumes fade away as we lose ourselves in the landscape of the actor's face, exploring every nuance of expression, dowsing for emotion in the invisible depths behind the eyes.

The natural choice for capturing this inner space is a shot of nothing but the actor's face: the tight close-up. The rest of the world falls away, crowded out and blurry. At close range a lens has much less depth of focus so the nearby face stands in high relief against a tapestry of soft, amorphous blobs of color.

At some point, though, there is such a thing as too big. And the bigger the screen, the sooner that point is reached. When a face really fills the big screen, say from eyebrows to chin, it stops being a face and becomes a graphic device, menacing perhaps in its abstraction but not a conduit for genuine emotion. Like the series of extreme close-ups of 365 pairs of bare buttocks in Yoko Ono's *Bottoms*, the face becomes nothing more than wiggly lines.

The inner landscape is as susceptible to light as the outer world, but here instead of defining space, light defines mood. Overall, the "look" of a picture can create emotional expectations, as in the shadowy *film noir* movies of the forties or the gritty *Taxi Driver* with its tough grainy feel, the brooding sunlit smog of *Blade Runner*, the glossy mythic sheen of *The Natural* or *The Color Purple*. The look creates an emotional space that allows for a certain range of emotional response. In the bright, scrubbed world of *The Natural*, men don't take their dates to porno films; in the grimy washed-out fluorescence of *Taxi Driver* they do. Critics objected to the sunny brilliance of *The Color Purple*, and it did seem odd that a tale of brutality and incest should look like a story from Uncle Remus, but you can be sure it was a calculated decision on Spielberg's part. This will not be a grim, depressing movie, he was saying; this will be a joyous celebration of life. Though some reviewers felt his choice compromised the original intentions of the novel, his message got through to audiences.

Light playing over a face shapes its emotional landscape. Harsh hard light creates stark, often menacing features, especially if it comes from below; soft diffuse light has a more romantic effect. Directors try to stage scenes so the lighting reflects the mood of the characters. When Talia Shire gets married at the beginning of *The Godfather* the scenes are bright and lush; when Al Pacino sits alone at the end of *The Godfather, Part II*, fulfilling the destiny he despised, he sits in dim, cold light.

The close-up is a seductive tool and can easily be overused. The size of the face in the frame is a message to the viewer: the bigger the close-up, the more important the moment. If the film is shot in loose singles, then jumping into a tight close-up for a climactic moment has almost shock value, as it jerks the viewer inside the character. But if the audience has been staring at big heads for the whole movie, another one means nothing. If the film is shot all in

big heads, what will the director use for the crucial scene? Good directors calibrate their shots, building a visual structure to parallel the emotional structure of the story.

If a moment is important, closing in can heighten it, but a director can't make a moment important by closing in. If the audience doesn't want to move in closer, to feel the moment magnified, it will feel manipulated by the director's trick. The audience will be pulled out of the picture. Like good Hollywood camera work, good Hollywood editing is invisible—we don't notice it because we are where we want to be. It feels as if we are the ones making the choices. When I watch a Roman Polanski film for the editing—Polanski is a superb editor—I soon find I have lost track of his cuts because his instinct for what I want to see is so sure I have stopped noticing his choices. This sort of obvious simplicity takes great craft

and considerable art. The result on the screen can be very impressionistic, as in Hitchcock's famous sequences, but the real trick is to be following the audience and leading it at the same time.

Editors and directors like singles for practical reasons. If a scene between two people is shot exclusively from one angle (say a "two-shot," a master angle that includes both characters more or less equally), their hands are tied. They can choose the take with the best overall effect and they can trim the beginning and end of the scene, but that's all they can do. They cannot shorten the scene by cutting a piece from the middle, and they cannot use the good part of one take and switch to the good part of another because joining two discontinuous pieces shot from the same camera angle creates an unacceptable glitch—slight differences in the character's positions, what is called a "jump cut." Often the director and the editor

The romance of soft light, the menace of hard
LEFT: Meryl Streep in *The French Lieutenant's Woman*, RIGHT: Jack Nicholson in *Chinatown*

have to make painful compromises on performance, sacrificing the beginning of the scene, which is better in one take, for the end, which is better in another, or picking the take that favors one actor's performance at the expense of another's.

But if the same scene is shot in singles (or "over-the-shoulder" shots where one of the actors is only a lumpy shoulder in the foreground), the editor and the director can almost redirect the scene on film. Because they are cutting back and forth, they are not locked into one choice for the whole. They can select absolutely the best performance for each actor at each moment; they can even completely drop out awkward parts of the scene.

But there is a price. After a while, too many close-ups disorient the voyeuristic eye—we feel claustrophobic or, worse, confused. And even in empathic terms too many singles, even carefully calibrated ones, ultimately weaken a film. Singles isolate the characters. If we spend too much time on one, we lose touch with the others. On the most practical level editors worry about "keeping a character alive," making sure everyone is seen often enough that the audience doesn't forget what they are doing or feeling in the scene. On a deeper level the scene photographed in singles can sacrifice the empathic resonance characters bring to each other's moments. Most scenes, after all, are about the effect people have on each other; if we are with one character too long we lose track of the other side of the human equation and thus the point of the scene.

Too much cutting back and forth, however, is disorienting. It takes time for viewers to register a new shot and reenter the mind of the new character. If the editor cuts too fast, the moments have no impact; worse, the audience senses it is being shown what it is supposed to look at, not what it wants to see. The audience thinks it is being told what to feel and resents it. This pulls the audience out of the picture, and the movie dies.

In dramatic moments the solid world of set and costume may fade away, but the space between the characters is charged with tension. Our culture has certain norms of social distance, certain rules we adhere to unconsciously when we confront each other. If someone comes closer, we automatically back off; if they are too far away we move in. If two men are arguing, exactly how they face off is an important cue to their intensity. If lovers are seducing each other, we are waiting for their clinch—whether or not we get it, the space between them is almost a third character, drawing them together.

This space can be created with certain techniques that maintain the advantages of the single. One way is to vary the sizes of the close-ups, shooting the woman's face big and the man's smaller, say, as he would look from her perspective. If we want to throw the emphasis on the larger character, make the audience feel the scene through her eyes, this can be very effective, emotionally weighting the space between them even as it defines it. If the scene should not be tilted toward one of the actors, directors sometimes prefer to shoot matching over-the-shoulder shots, where we concentrate on one actor with the other's back still in the frame. The presence of both actors' bodies keeps them connected while the editor retains the freedom to cut for performance since only one actor's face is visible at a time.

But in most love scenes, for instance, we don't want to see the scene only from one character's point of view, and we don't want a Cary Grant or an Ingrid Bergman to be just a dark lump in the foreground. So, important as singles are, editors have another saying, "The best shot of all is a two-shot that works." If the scene doesn't need to be fiddled with, if the director caught both actors in peak performance on the same take, at a rhythm that feels true but not self-indulgent, there is nothing better. Even an editor with the instincts of an actor, who can build a scene from singles to match the rhythms of life, can never match the quirky vitality of actors playing off each other. The actors' work will have a hidden rightness about it beyond the editor's formula, experience, or even instinct. Better yet, the editor isn't telling you where to look. The audience switches at will from person to person. No little moment is too short to notice, no actor is forcibly ignored, the viewer never feels manipulated. If the shot works, the empathic rhythms are so sure in the writing, the performance, and the staging that the viewer is wafted along effortlessly from moment to moment.

Comedy scenes that rely for their effect on natural timing are as inviolable as a single moment; they almost have to play in an unbroken master shot. *The Philadelphia Story*, for instance, is a masterpiece of two-shots. Close-ups are only used to punctuate important moments; otherwise, the movie is a series of scenes shot in masters, almost a textbook collection of two-shots that work. Woody Allen felt so strongly about the importance of real interplay for his humor in *Annie Hall* that he had Gordon Willis devise ways to shoot as single shots, even special-effects scenes that use split-screen and ghost images so all the characters could interact. And Allen views cutting into close-up for the punch line as a crude way of underlining, and undermining, the joke.

Remember the moment of sweet revenge in *Annie Hall* when Allen has to wait in line next to a self-styled media expert (Russell Horton) and can't contain his contempt for the man's pretentious remarks about Marshall McLuhan? Horton overhears Allen's barbs and puts him down by saying he's a professor of media at Columbia, at which point Allen leads him just beyond the frame—and there is McLuhan himself, who tells the man he's a pompous twit. Before McLuhan is revealed there is a full two and a half minutes of dialogue, counterpoint between the professor's pontifications and a discussion of Allen's sexual problems with Diane Keaton. This is a very long scene to shoot from a single angle, and certainly the easiest and most efficient way to do it would have been to choose a new angle at least for the final joke, the unveiling of McLuhan. Then if McLuhan, not exactly a pro at stand-up comedy, muffs his lines he hasn't ruined the whole scene; only his part of it has to be reshot.

But Allen wouldn't do that. He felt the humor depended on filming the scene as a single continuous shot, so when we discover McLuhan he's actually been waiting there, for real, during the whole first part of the scene. Allen pays a price—McLuhan's line is stilted and garbled (it sounds as if he says,". . . you mean my whole fallacy is wrong"), but the trade-off is worth it. Knowing McLuhan is there, at Allen's beck and call, to put down the boorish media expert is more important than his exact line reading. Audience laughter covers the line anyway. As Woody Allen says to end the scene, "Boy, if life were only like this."

Most first-rate directors plan their cutting patterns before they shoot. They are willing to gamble on a two-shot if it is right for the moment and if they are confident their actors can deliver, but they

Sweet revenge in *Annie Hall*

also know when to narrow their focus. If the scene allows, they will let the characters themselves "motivate the coverage," that is, seem to make the director's choices for him. A director might stage a conversation, as Pakula does in *All the President's Men,* so the characters' movements naturally bring them together for a two-shot and split them apart when it feels right for singles. Here Pakula has the best of both worlds—the voyeuristic eye is watching a scene well grounded in geometric space, since following the characters back and forth gives us a good, clear sense of where they are and how they're positioned with respect to each other, and the vicarious eye is where it wants to be in the empathic space, since it is the heat of their discussion that draws the actors together into the same frame or pulls them apart to stand by themselves.

Dangerous Liaisons shows the strengths and weaknesses of working with a much more limited palette. The film is as carefully planned as *Annie Hall* and *The Philadelphia Story,* but it is laid out in a string of singles, punctuated with barely enough wider shots to set the action and give some flavor of pre-Revolutionary France. The director (Stephen Frears) frames so tight that a normal single feels loose and airy by comparison. Even his two-shots are often so close that they function as singles—at that distance only one of the characters is in focus at a time, and when the emphasis shifts back and forth the focus shifts with it, so they take turns as fuzzy blobs in the frame. Instead of saving the big climactic close-up, Frears uses it in every major scene.

The resulting film can at times be wearing and annoyingly claustrophobic. Yet it takes on a special intensity that suits its particular subject. *Dangerous Liaisons* is about two jaded connoisseurs of emotion, decadent parasites whose only pleasure is manipulating the feelings of others without ever being touched themselves. They feel superior, invulnerable, but in the end they are marooned souls, trapped in their emotional isolation. The big close-up is the perfect shot to convey this sense of emotional quarantine. Its nature isolates the characters within themselves. By choosing the big close-up the director is saying, "This film is not about what goes on between these characters but what goes on within them." What matters for the characters, and for us, is the delicious frisson of irony they get from saying what they don't feel—whether it's an outright lie or a double entendre—and the pleasure they derive from the moral conflicts they cause in others. As the Malkovich character says about his seduction of the virtuous Michelle Pfeiffer, he doesn't want her to abandon her principles, he wants to savor her inner struggle between virtue and desire. That sort of inner struggle is what big close-ups show best.

Big close-ups not only isolate, they can make us feel manipulated, since the director is telling us exactly what to look at. This story, however, is about manipulation. In this case the choreographed jumping from character to character seems contrived not by the director but by the characters themselves, as they stage-manage their own scenes. We are seeing what the manipulative characters would want us to see, and it works just fine.

There is a price. As the story progresses, all Malkovich's cool manipulation can't protect him from falling in love for real. But by now, the insistent use of big close-ups has so compartmentalized each character's emotions, made them so calculated and selfishly personal, that finally when real contact is supposed to take place we

Dangerous Liaisons

don't feel it. Now we yearn for the spontaneity of an honest relationship. We want to watch the actors play off each other without the director knowing who to be on in advance; we want a shot where we can choose who to look at. But the stylistic choices that define the look of the film make that impossible. The director's mix captures every nuance of private feeling, but it cannot convince us of the impromptu truth of shared emotion.

Rain Man, which won the Best Picture Oscar *Dangerous Liaisons* was nominated for, is also a vicarious film, not heavy with plot or action but built around the inner lives of its two main characters. But it was shot in a diametrically opposite way. As Ken Zunder, camera operator on the film, put it, "It's a film about two brothers, about their relationship. It was clear to anyone who read the script that we had to keep both of them in the same frame as much as possible."

Rain Man

The film is dominated by two-shots. When the brothers are sitting by a duck pond, for example, and Tom Cruise is trying to talk Dustin Hoffman into coming to Los Angeles ("Hey, Fernando is pitching on Wednesday"), the pair is photographed from the side in a tight two-shot, almost like the extra-large two-shots in *Dangerous Liaisons*. Both are even taken with a telephoto lens so the backgrounds will be an out-of-focus blur and our attention will bore in on the characters. But there is a crucial difference. In *Rain Man* both faces stay in focus for the whole scene so we can watch the brothers interact moment to moment. In a later scene, when Cruise is on the telephone at the airport and we see Hoffman in the background watching television, he's not a mere blur but held painstakingly in focus by use of a split diopter, a special half-lens placed in front of the camera to let it focus on two planes at once. The film is about the chains of love and pain that bind a man to his brother. It is only fitting that two should be bound together in the frame.

INVISIBLE MUSIC

The vicarious world, a place of shifting emphasis, of subterranean rhythms, of all the subtlety and complexity of emotional nuance, is the place where theater and music converge. Both film and opera bring them together, but while the drama serves the music in an opera, in a movie it is the other way around. Background music has occasionally been tried in plays, but it rarely works; the effect is absurdly artificial, like plastic flowers at a funeral. Yet the chances are that all the emotional high points of your favorite Hollywood films were underscored with music. Somehow, since the actors are so much larger than life and pasted on a wall, since their softest whispers are broadcast by massive speaker arrays, a delicate overlay of music feels almost natural.

I am not talking about the big music, the great movie themes like "Lara's Theme" from *Dr. Zhivago*, or the *Star Wars* music, or the theme to *The Bridge on the River Kwai* or *The Magnificent Seven*. These are the province of spectacle, and in the voyeuristic world they share an equal status with the panoramic shot as an epic statement of the essence of a film. Some films, like *Chariots of Fire*, are nothing but a big score (if you doubt me, try running it without the sound). But most movie music, in fact the most important music from the filmmaker's point of view, should never be heard.

Sound mixers have such pinpoint control over the relative sound levels and music can be so precisely placed that properly used it is invisible, a magic pixie dust that intensifies the emotions and evaporates.

Composer Arnold Schoenberg agreed to score a film once if he could tell the actors exactly how to pitch their lines. He got it backward. The able film composer must be as sensitive to performance as a film editor and take as much pride in serving the story. If the composer captures the mood of the piece exactly, he will lift the scene and waft it along; if he gets it wrong, the scene will have to sail into his wind. Sometimes the composer can wreck the scene completely, as in Natalie Wood's big angry office scene in *The Cracker Factory*—one of her best moments as an actress—which is completely smashed by a heavy-handed score of forced and obvious emotion that betrays the intensity and honesty of her performance.

How much music and where to put it is to some extent a matter of convention. To the modern ear, many forties movies (almost any scored by Max Steiner or many of Bernard Herrmann's that weren't for Hitchcock, for instance) feel music-heavy. Recently the practice of profuse and insistent scoring has been revived to cater to the music video generation. But even directors who aren't worrying about spinning off an album lean on the score.

Once a film is substantially edited, the director normally runs it with the composer and "spots the score," that is, tells the composer where the movie needs music. They discuss the nature of the music —will there be a love theme, for instance, or does the villain have a sound signature, and, above all, what is the general architecture of the piece? Perhaps the love turns sour; how should the music reflect that? Music is hard to describe, however, and unless the director is a trained composer, chances are he is going to be surprised. Recording a full orchestra is viciously expensive, but it is not unthinkable to have a movie scored two or three times or even more; *Reds* had an entire Stephen Sondheim score that never made the film, and the Joe Jackson score on the sound-track album for *Mike's Murder* was substantially replaced by John Barry between the time the album came out and the film was released.

Directors often think they won't use music they spot, but they order it to be on the safe side. Unless they're in trouble, they're likely to tell themselves that scenes play fine without it. Yet usually by the time the film is finished there is much more music than the director planned on, because once the music is in place the director realizes how much more juice it gives the scenes. It seems the right music makes us feel more intensely than we thought we could.

Like the voyeur's world, the vicarious world thrives on a delicate balance between expectation and surprise. We are not feeling our own emotions but someone else's. We want them to be richer and more intense than our own. We don't fully trust the borrowed feelings if they don't give us something we didn't expect, something we couldn't bring to the experience ourselves. If, in casting, a director comments about an actor, as is directors' wont, "He's okay, but there are no surprises," you know the director has found the actor of last resort—good enough perhaps to sturdily support a tight story but lacking any special quality that will bring life to the picture, that will animate the screen.

The main advantage of film over life is that in film you can repeat things until they're done exactly right, first in the crunch of shooting and then with calm reflection in the editing room. The system allows, even demands, maniacal perfectionism. Think of the famous moment in *Jezebel* when Bette Davis uses her riding crop to hitch up her skirt, a gesture of gay insouciance which only came off on the forty-fifth take. The production manager of *The Parallax View* still has a slate in his office marked "Take 98–Warren stirs soup."

Since once something is committed to film it happens every time, films achieve a magical perfection to which it would be folly for theater to aspire. This gives us the glories of a Chaplin routine, but it also leads to the ruthless excesses of directors, who know they only have to get it right once and they'll have it forever. For a key scene in *A Tree Grows in Brooklyn*, for example, director Elia Kazan writes in *A Life* that he convinced young Peggy Ann Garner that her real-life father, an air force flyer, wasn't coming home alive:

> Peggy cried the whole day through and we caught that piece of feeling. We only got it once, but we only needed it once. Her outburst of pain and fear was essential to her performance. It was the real thing.

Many actors and actresses older than Garner collude in this. They hate being manipulated, but they are proud of the end result, and given the choice they would do it again. If the result is good enough, they tell themselves, it was worth the pain and humiliation or they wouldn't be actors.

Because movie moments only have to happen once, an undisciplined, totally unpredictable but vital presence can inhabit the screen. Marilyn Monroe as a legitimate stage actress is inconceivable; Monroe as a movie actress may have been impossible to work with, she may have sacrificed the best work of all around her to get her own, but she lights up the dead screen with the gift of life. And that is the vital essence of the vicarious film experience.

THE VISCERAL EYE

ARNHEIM'S SQUARE

Look at the dot in the square. Arnheim says in *Art and Visual Perception* that your eye will quickly tell you it is off-center. This is not a judgment of the intellect because it does not rely on abstract concepts, and it is not an emotional judgment, since the off-centeredness might arouse different emotions in different people. Visual judgment is an immediate and indispensable part of the act of seeing itself. Seeing the dot off-center is an intrinsic part of seeing it at all.

Look at the dot, Arnheim maintains, and you will see it exhibits a quality beyond its size and location—restlessness. You will feel a tension pulling it toward the center of the square. This too is as much a part of seeing the dot as its size and shape. Notice that it is the dot that seems to be pulled into place by the square, not the square by the dot. The square provides a boundary, a frame, and within a frame our eye imposes certain innate rules. It tries to organize what it sees, it tries for balance, it tries to see the frame as a whole. Art depends for its effect, Arnheim maintains, on this kind of perceptual trick of the brain.

Take away the square, then. What do you have? No longer an art object—no more a work complete in itself, defined by its own boundaries—but part of our everyday world. A ball or a blot on the page but not a composition.

OPPOSITE PAGE
INSET: *The Wild Bunch*,
LEFT: *One Million Years B.C.*

Take away the screen frame and the same thing happens to a movie. Yet from the silent films of Abel Gance through Cinerama people have tried to break down the barrier between us and what we're watching. If three-dimensional space is so important, they argue, then the more three-dimensional the better. What better way to put us inside the screen than to literally do just that?

Imax is the current final solution. Shown in fifty-five specially constructed theaters around the world, the Imax film frame is the largest ever, ten times the size of the thirty-five-millimeter standard, throwing the largest, sharpest, brightest big-screen picture of all time on screens as much as seven stories high and wider than peripheral vision. Combined with state-of-the-art six-channel stereo sound, the results are literally mind-boggling. As a producer once said, your eyes make a party for your head.

It is the ultimate voyeuristic experience—you *are* there. NASA sent an Imax camera on the space shuttle and released the footage as a film. It is as close to being in space as you are likely to get. For me, drifting along, watching the earth turning below, the title was truer than they knew: *The Dream Is Alive.*

I wrote a film for Greg MacGillivray, one of the masters of Imax, a precise, careful technician (the medium demands technical mastery) and a gifted cameraman-director who pioneered the surfing film and perfected the helicopter shot. We ran some of his Imax films, first on video and then at an Imax theater, so he could explain the peculiarities of what is arguably the world's most technically advanced film medium, the closest we've come to pure movie.

ABOVE: Standard 35mm, RIGHT: IMAX

What I learned was that this Gargantua is a primitive. The images have such presence and power that they are a whole new experience. This is what it must have felt like to be present at the creation, to see the very first films. Words shrivel in the immensity. To tell my story I wouldn't be writing words, I would be writing images in the style of the classic silent movie.

But unlike silent films the sheer size and power of the images are a narrow straitjacket for the form. Since the screen extends beyond peripheral vision there is effectively no frame, so composition in the conventional sense ceases to exist. The verticals and horizontals don't relate to a rectangular whole, as in a painting or conventional film; as in life, the image dribbles off around the edges. To maintain the peripheral image effect the eye has to be kept centered, so any meaningful action must take place in the bottom third of the frame, near the middle. To enhance the effect, a sense of depth is crucial; for his gigantic films MacGillivray tries to have his backgrounds lighter than his foregrounds, just as Eames did in his tiny films of children's toys.

A scene cannot be shot in close-ups—not only will the head be huge beyond any emotional significance but the images are so present, their world so real, that it is profoundly disorienting to break into a scene by changing to another angle in the middle. Without the frame, you really do feel each cut as a dizzying leap through space, just as the first filmmakers had feared.

In practice, only four kinds of shots work in Imax: breathtaking long shots; somewhat less breathtaking medium shots, which perform the storytelling function of the medium and close shots in regular film; breathtaking macro close-ups—showstopping graphic effects like a butterfly the size of a house; and point-of-view shots, the real payoff of an Imax film.

Point-of-view shots, or POVs, show us what things look like from the perspective of someone or something in the scene. If we are shown the heroine tied to the railroad tracks, for example, we might see the onrushing train from her point of view and her body coming closer from the train's. POV shots show us the scene not as an objective event watched from outside by a dispassionate camera but from the inside as part of the action. Point-of-view shots put us in the picture, which is what Imax is all about. But that isn't why they are so crucial to the medium.

Most people, it seems, don't see Imax movies for sheer voyeuristic delight. How many subjects are as voyeuristically compelling as

OVERLEAF
POV from *To the Limit* in IMAX

outer space? The POV shot adds another dimension: gut-grabbing thrills. Since the screen extends beyond peripheral vision and the image is so sharp and bright, when you fly through the Grand Canyon or race a car at two hundred miles an hour the rush is positively stomach-churning.

This is no vicarious pleasure. As long as the sensation of moving into the screen is artfully created—by having vertical objects like trees flash by or the rim of a canyon fall away below, for example —it doesn't matter who is having the experience. It might not even be a person, it might be a dummy on a rocket sled or a bird. The point here is not to feel what the character feels but to feel your own emotions, to have the experience yourself, directly.

Here, the viewer's relation with the character is reversed—the character is a conduit for the viewer's feelings, not the other way around. When we watch a roller-coaster sequence in a movie, how much of the thrill comes from seeing the riders act scared and sharing their emotions, and how much comes from experiencing the ride ourselves? Which would be more effective, only shots of the screaming riders or only POV shots of the rails rushing up at us as we dive and twist and turn? Are we watching the riders to see who is sick, who is excited? No. They aren't characters in the em-pathic sense, they are cheerleaders for *our* roller-coaster ride, there to intensify our thrill of motion, but more likely than not they just get in the way.

No Imax film is complete without two or three gut-wrenching POVs. Even *The Dream Is Alive* had a gratuitous (and after the *Challenger* disaster, sadly ironic) high-speed slide down an escape rope. Imax films are beautiful, they cost millions, they are techni-cally superb, they are high-minded documentaries shown in science-museum theaters, but they owe their enormous audience success to the cheap thrills of a roller coaster. Which they deliver in spades.

Visceral thrills are filmmaking's dirty little secret. Though they can require considerable art to achieve, there is nothing artistic about the results—the passions aroused are not lofty, they're the gut reactions of the lizard brain—thrill of motion, joy of destruc-tion, lust, blood lust, terror, disgust. Sensations, you might say, rather than emotions. More complex feelings require the empathic process, but these simple, powerful urges reach out and grab us by the throat without an intermediary. When people find something in a movie offensive (as opposed to stupid or boring or phony), whether it's the slow-motion killing in *The Wild Bunch*, the monster in *The Fly*, or the blatant titillation of soft-core porn, it's getting them on the visceral level. It stirs something inside them that they find repulsive. Other people, of course, savor the tingle.

While the morality of stirring the beast is debatable, visceral sensation in one form or another slithers like a serpent through all Hollywood films. The gifted director can find a place for it in the explosive moments of any genre. There are times we like to share the emotions of the characters, and there are times we want the character to be *us*, when we want to experience the moment directly. We surrender to it in the horror film, the porno film, the action movie, but it also flavors the adventure film, the thriller. Love stories completely devoid of titillation are very weak tea. Detective stories trade in it when, in Raymond Chandler's words, they "evoke the smell of fear."

We are in a primal, personal world here, buried deep within, a world where sights and sounds trigger life-and-death responses. What feels real here is not the plausible, as in the voyeur's world, not the emotionally true of the vicarious world, but the thrill—the way your gut twinges when you see a flashing red light in your

The Fly

Barbarella

rearview mirror, the surge in your loins a beautiful body stirs, the sickening sense that tonight your dreams will be nightmares. It feels real because it is real: it is happening to you. The fundamental criticism in the voyeur's world is "that couldn't happen," in the vicarious world "he wouldn't do that," but in the visceral world it is "it doesn't get me."

Visceral kicks are more purely cinematic than the sedate rewards of the voyeur or the vicarious eye. Theater cannot put you up on the stage; novels can only produce indirectly through words what films mainline straight into the subconscious as images. While film catches only the shadow of a great literary character, a Raskolnikov, it makes a bloodthirsty, insect-bodied alien more terrifyingly evocative than anything on the page.

Good acting can help but is not essential. The actor, like the riders in the roller-coaster sequence, performs a limited role. He is a placeholder for the viewer. Simply by being there he allows the viewer to project himself into the scene. When I watch a rock climber scale Yosemite's Half Dome without a rope my stomach drops out. I sweat ice. If the climber felt what I feel, he would be mashed to hamburger by the rocks below. The baby-sitter being stalked or Rambo wreaking revenge may or may not be empathic vehicles for us—that is, we may or may not enter into what the actors are feeling—but even if we don't, we can still feel the terror or the blood lust of the moment. If the camera dwells too long on their faces and the empathic response begins to take over, we might even feel impatient for more of the meat of the scene.

One would expect the point-of-view shot to be a good way to get inside a character's head, on the theory that if we see what the character sees, we will feel what the character feels. But in practice it doesn't work that way. We need to see the actor's face to trigger our vicarious response. The POV by itself doesn't give us any emotional clues about how the character is reacting or story clues about what he is going to do next. Blended well with shots of the actor— say, in the chase sequence in *The French Connection* or in classic Hitchcock—the POV can give us a peculiarly vibrant sensation of being inside the character's skin, but the exact mix is crucial to the effect. Liberally interspersed with the right close-ups, as in the shower scene in *Psycho*, the POV can have devastating impact by blending our gut emotions into our empathic feelings for the character. Used in longer takes with fewer interruptions the POV can be a roller-coaster ride in its own right, merely spiced by the char-

acter's reactions, like the chase scene in *Bullitt* or the skiing sequences in *Downhill Racer*.

One of Hollywood's most fascinating failures is *Lady in the Lake*, a Robert Montgomery film based on a Raymond Chandler story and shot entirely from the point of view of the main character. We *are* Philip Marlowe. We only see Marlowe when we look in a mirror. When we light a cigarette, smoke curls in front of the lens. People threaten and cajole us in the best Chandler fashion; we crack wise and get punched out. A bold concept, well produced, but a flop on the screen. The POV puts us in the scene, but it doesn't put us in the hero's head, it puts us in his shoes, and unless something pretty spectacular is going on that is not a very thrilling place to be.

The POV shot isn't the only gateway to the visceral world. For my rock climber I don't need a POV shot to get my chills. A swaying shot of the ground from his position might help, or it might intrude. It might feel contrived—to get that shot the camera had to get there

A point of view from *The Lady in the Lake*. This is a production still; in the film, Robert Montgomery's right hand would be on the right side of the frame.

somehow, and if some poor cameraman laden with equipment can scale Half Dome, how hard can it be for a climber wearing nothing but a bag of chalk and bathing trunks?

The most telling shot, the money shot in my climbing sequence, will be the shot that delivers maximum thrill value. It will have to make the climbing look extremely dangerous and absolutely un-fakeable. My climber will have to be doing a particularly hazardous maneuver, and he will have to be seen from an angle that shows him large enough to watch but small enough that I can see how far he has to fall. The best angle would probably be looking down from above with the distant rocks beneath. The next best would be from below, if there is a good stretch of sheer rock between him and the bottom of the frame. Close-ups, so powerful for intensifying the vicarious impact of the actor's emotions, only diminish the visceral because in close-ups the danger is no longer real and palpable. Creating the thrilling effect is as much a matter of optics and camera angles as of real jeopardy. If our climber risking his life was never filmed to show the danger—if the cameraman cropped the mountain off below him or shot him only in close-ups—he might as well have been climbing a ten-foot wall.

Unlike the sweeping vistas of voyeuristic spectacle, the thrill shot is slow to pall. Eventually, danger without disaster loses its edge (if it's so dangerous why hasn't he fallen yet?), but as long as the thrill lasts, the shot holds. Especially if the climber isn't using a rope.

Smart producers will do whatever it takes to create these crucial shots. The most complicated shot in *Indiana Jones and the Temple of Doom*, and no doubt among the most expensive, was just such a shot of the heroes hanging from the edge of a cliff. Nobody risked his life, of course. George Lucas's special-effects company, Industrial Light & Magic, combined over thirty different elements optically to create the ultimate cliffhanger, the payoff shot designed to show off our heroes' desperate predicament seen from above so it looks as if lives are really at stake.

Speed stirs the beast. Fast-paced action and a hustling camera suck the thrill seeker in us into a scene. Here the camera is the star —the way it is used is just as important for creating the sensation of speed as what happens on the set. Well shot, a bicycle ride can be as exciting as an Indianapolis 500 (and a poorly shot Indianapolis 500 can feel like a bicycle ride).

As the car is our national icon of speed and freedom, many a film is burdened with a gratuitous car chase in hopes of triggering the gut response, and every cameraman has his ploys for squeezing

OPPOSITE PAGE
A telephoto lens puts the truck hot on Michael Douglas' heels in *Black Rain*.

the most juice from it, worked out by careful experimentation so the audience will not sense the tricks. Car POVs (shots of the road rushing up at us) may be shot low to the ground so the blacktop speeds past closer to camera; with a wide-angle lens, which has the effect of accelerating movement nearer the camera; off-speed, at twenty or twenty-two frames per second instead of twenty-four, to speed up the movement; with the sun at a certain angle, to take advantage of the strobing effect of shadows. If a car must make a dangerous maneuver, weaving in and out of traffic, a telephoto lens will enhance the effect by compressing space, stacking up the cars on top of each other. But too strong a telephoto and our eyes aren't fooled.

We can be fooled, but we mustn't feel fooled. The visceral world is very unforgiving of stunts and special effects that feel hokey so Hollywood has finely honed these skills. Ironically, though, theatrical films must also be perceived as make-believe. We would be appalled to think a stuntman died for our amusement. In making *Comes a Horseman*, for instance, a stuntman died in a freak accident doing what should have been a simple trick. I saw the footage. It was innocuous in that the fatal take was no more gruesome than the other takes, and there was some talk of using the original as a tribute of sorts to the late stuntman, but it was never seriously countenanced. To indulge in the visceral thrill of the fatal stunt was obscene, even though it was indistinguishable from the other takes. It made me feel like a psychopathic ghoul. Not only did it pull me out of the picture, it made me question my whole response to stunt footage. We can pander to our visceral side, it seems, as long as we know it's all in fun.

Just as the voyeuristic eye becomes bored, the visceral eye becomes jaded. A threshold must be passed for the visceral thrill to kick in, and the more seasoned the viewer the higher that is, as if thrills were a form of drug to which we develop a tolerance. Plots are no cleverer, characters are no deeper or subtler than they were fifty years ago, but if Sylvester Stallone downs a helicopter with an arrow in *Rambo: First Blood Part II*, he has to ram it with a tank in *Rambo III*.

In the visceral sequence the cameraman, the stunt coordinator, and the special-effects technicians come into their own, and assistant directors (the set managers who love the challenges of intricate planning) rise to the occasion with relish. But for a director interested in character and story, shooting these sequences is boring, time-consuming, and repetitive. Visceral sequences demand complex traffic direction rather than skill with actors, and they often depend on temperamental and dangerous special effects such as explosions and car crashes. These scenes often require many cameras filming at once or high-speed cameras that slow the action so much the director cannot possibly imagine what they are catching. Movie sets are notorious for long hours of idleness waiting on technicians, but even for a movie set these sequences generate a great deal of standing around, things going wrong, and nervous asking of specialists if they got it all right.

Yet if a director likes to play with film—and many of the most skilled directors including Steven Spielberg and Orson Welles have said they love the feeling of being a grown-up kid playing with a giant toy—the visceral scenes are their pride and joy. This has more to do with the nature of the visceral experience than with all the paraphernalia they get to command. These are the scenes where the medium is most plastic, where the director has the most freedom to indulge his or her subjective side. Though apparently at the mercy of technicians, if the director knows his stuff this is where he is king, free from cajoling actors, free from the demands of the story, free from rigid rules of time and space.

The director, however, isn't given a license for random self-indulgence. The aim is to create a particular gut reaction in the audience. And in order to achieve the effect the director must look deep inside, not to plumb the subtleties of emotion but to re-create the way the world looks to a person under stress. The director comes face to face with the subjective quality of lived experience. Instead of the voyeur's outer world of objective geometric space or the vicarious inner world of emotions, the visceral is the outer world distorted by our inner passions, twisted by the pressure of our own excited emotions pushing against our senses.

The test for the visceral eye is a test of emotional truth, but it does not depend on the actor's ability to convey honest emotion—it is a test of the director's ability to re-create his or her own raw feelings directly inside the viewer's head. It is filmmaking at its most personal, and that it has such power over the viewer is testimony to the fundamental commonality of human experience. Time and space may warp, but they warp in ways we all recognize, or Hollywood films would be cult art.

Take the climax of *Bonnie and Clyde*, where Arthur Penn riddles his characters with bullets, pioneering the much-maligned innovation of slow-motion gore. From a visceral point of view, slow motion has the advantage of stretching out the thrill, giving us more bang for the buck. But that is the least of it. The power of Penn's images means he strikes much deeper. Extending the moment captures the "uh-oh," the awful space between knowing and feeling an irrevocable disaster—between tripping and falling, between dropping something and hearing it smash, between losing the car in a skid and hitting the wall.

Apparently, we stretch out that moment in the living of it, or Penn's innovation would have remained a mere curiosity instead of the movie staple it has become. But Penn didn't invent the slow-motion action scene so much as apply a standard technique for explosions and stunts to the portrayal of carnage, overlaying the visceral thrill of blood lust with the gut twinge of the "uh-oh." He was showing us new meaning in the gut shock of violence.

By now, the slow-motion payoff is such a Hollywood commonplace that it is losing its visceral power. Once it becomes a convention, a formula derived from other movies rather than lived experience, it becomes something to watch rather than something to feel. Now, when we watch the climactic moment of *Jules and Jim* and see Jeanne Moreau drive off a bridge in real time instead of gracefully soaring in slow-mo it comes as a refreshing shock. Truffaut reminds us that disaster can strike before we even know what's happening. His vision too has perceptual truth—his visceral moment is as jolting and unforgettable as Penn's.

VISCERAL TIME AND SPACE

Visceral space isn't picture-pretty. In a space designed to envelop, laws of artistic composition become trivial. Instead of static framing, the space is defined by sound and movement—action pulling us into the scene, sweeping us along, flashing by us, exploding in our face.

The actual images from the shower scene in *Psycho*, for instance —water coming from a shower head, a hand with a knife, parts of arms and torso—are in themselves mundane, poorly lit, even out of focus, and shot at odd angles from a spatial standpoint. But they add up to a visceral world of ambush and terror because through them Hitchcock re-creates for us the fragmented impressions of a murder victim. It is not exactly point-of-view any more than our thoughts are point-of-view; our thoughts, after all, include us in the scene, in some vaguely imagined way, just as Hitchcock includes

Janet Leigh. But each shot is not a composition to be studied, it's an impression, a beat of a rhythm. Movement is in the shots but it is also in the speed of the cuts themselves, in the "montage." Film-makers get excited by visceral cutting because the sum is so much greater than the parts—a few simple shots put together right drop us into a world of urgent, overpowering intensity. Paintings give us spectacle, novels give us story and character, theater gives us great performances, but only film can provide the visceral satisfactions of montage.

In the voyeur's universe, wide shots and clever staging create the impression that there is life beyond the boundaries of the screen; in the visceral universe, that off-screen space, that part of the scene we don't see, can be more powerful than what we do see. In the world of perception distorted by emotion, where our imaginations are so actively involved in shaping what we're seeing, once the imagination is primed our own fantasies take over. In the *Psycho* scene, we never see the knife cut flesh (see the shower sequence on pp. 140–141).

Where space distorts, time too is plastic. When a crisis floods our senses things seem to happen hopelessly fast or agonizingly slow. In the vicarious experience we have a finely tuned sense of natural time, in the voyeur's we have an inner urge to step up the pace a little, but in visceral space there is no metronome beating inside us, no irreducible unit of time, no story beat or actor's moment. Here time stretches and shrinks to fit the inner twinge of the gut. What propels the experience forward isn't the voyeur's compression of action or the vicarious tension of dramatic conflict, it is "suspense" —in its original sense of action temporarily interrupted. Tweaking the visceral urge, then backing off; teasing the lizard brain.

Just as visceral space is defined by movement, visceral time is defined by rhythms. Action by itself, no matter how frenetic or skillfully portrayed, palls; to keep the freshness of surprise, move-ment needs to ebb and flow. The editor's job cutting in visceral time is to sense these rhythms, to pace the action, speeding it up for maximum impact, then slowing it down, lulling, even maddening with inactivity, only to surprise again with action. Once we see the killer in the victim's bedroom he can take forever to reach her sleeping body.

The extreme examples of the visceral are the suspense scene and the action scene. The first consists of long, tantalizing pauses punc-tuated by sudden violent action; the second of violent action punc-tuated by pauses. Suspense scenes are usually shot in long, continuous takes; action scenes are chopped into many bits, the cutting itself propelling the action. Often the long, slow rhythms of a whole suspense sequence are used to set up the sudden burst of movement of a big action scene.

SUSPENSE

Suspense depends on foreknowledge. If we know the bomb is on the bus, the killer is in the room, the friction between what we expect to happen and what we hope will happen causes shivers in our spine. This is our sensation, not the actors'. They can share our anxiety, our suspense, as Audrey Hepburn in *Wait Until Dark* and the crew stalking the creature in *Alien* do, or they can be blissfully ignorant of the danger, innocent victims aboard a sabotaged plane.

Anxiety by itself isn't suspense. Anxiety has to rub against hope. It is not enough that there be a bomb on the plane, there has to be

Raiders of the Lost Ark

some chance that it will be discovered in time. As long as there is hope, we're watching a race and betting on the dark horse; otherwise, we're only witnessing a tragedy.

There are two basic kinds of visceral suspense, time suspense—will he get there in time? will they reach the bomb before it blows?—and space suspense —where is he? where did he put the bomb? Time suspense depends on having a confined time—some sort of deadline—space suspense depends on having a confined area. When Clint Eastwood stalks a killer in an empty warehouse, we're not waiting for a clock to tick down. We're peering into the dark corners with him, alert for the inevitable attack. The chill comes from knowing the killer is in there, somewhere, and the attack can come at any moment from anywhere. When Cary Grant searches the Nazi wine cellar in *Notorious* we know he's only safe until the Nazis come down for more champagne, and the thrill comes from knowing he's in a race against time and losing.

Just as it helps space suspense to have a defined spatial sequence —a row of aisles, say, which are searched one by one—so it helps time suspense to have a way of keeping time, of watching the sand as it trickles from the hourglass, particularly since time is so plastic in building the suspense sequence. In *Notorious* we are with Ingrid Bergman, upstairs at the party, counting the champagne bottles as they disappear, knowing that when they're gone Grant's time in the cellar is up. In *The Man Who Knew Too Much* the assassin is to strike during the crescendo of a symphony, when a cymbal crashes; amid all the action, while we listen to the music build, we watch the percussionist methodically prepare for the fatal moment.

Suspense thrives on more suspense. Among writers, producers, and directors it is a given that to build a taut sequence there should be more than one suspense element. In a formula picture like *Marooned*, it's not enough for NASA chief Gregory Peck to launch a completely untested rocket on impossibly short notice, he has to shoot it through the eye of a hurricane. In *Aliens* no sooner do the marines realize they're trapped by voracious monsters than they discover they're sitting on an atomic reactor about to go thermonuclear. (In both cases, the second element provides a ticking clock.)

While suspense scenes can take great liberties with time and space, they are helped by defining their own standards and sticking to them. We have to feel we are using up our options. It can take us five minutes to watch the last two minutes of a time bomb tick off, it can even take one minute for the first minute and four minutes for the last minute, but we need to refer back to a yardstick we can trust—to the timer on that bomb, an approaching guard, or vanishing champagne bottles. When a house is being searched, we want to know the searcher is closing in on the hiding place.

Generally, in building a time suspense sequence, time starts at a good clip and slows down in a sort of logarithmic curve. As the crisis nears, seconds stretch into minutes, lengthened by judiciously slowing the action but also by showing parallel action in series. The editor can actually repeat the same bit of time for all our suspense elements so in thirty seconds of jumping back and forth we see interwoven the last ten seconds in the life of the ticking bomb, the innocent victims, the frantic searchers. Often the effect is heightened by cutting back and forth faster and faster as the explosion gets closer, almost as our pulse quickens.

When it comes to spatial suspense, however, not much is gained by manipulating time. A sense of threat hangs over Clint Eastwood from the moment he enters the warehouse searching for the hidden killer. We can stretch out the moment, but what matters isn't how long he is taking but what is happening out beyond the edge of the screen. Clint walks, he searches—we're aching to see what is just beyond our view, certain that right out there, right behind Clint, where we can't quite see, the killer lurks. This effect is heightened if a scene is shot in extended, continuous takes that can be interrupted at any moment by sudden attack, as in *Alien* or *Wait Until Dark*. The long takes serve to unveil the space slowly but surely, bringing relief and tension at the same time, letting us feel exactly how much we've safely seen and how much is left to see.

Here, the editor and the director can heighten the suspense by violating their own basic rule and withholding what we want to see. When Clint searches, we're straining along with him to see what he sees—"what we want to be on" isn't Clint's squinty eyes but his squinty-eyed point of view. The editor can tease us by holding it back, leaving us to stare at Clint instead, trying to guess what he sees. Suspense is the thrill of anticipation.

Building anticipation builds up the pressure on the final explosive moment; as the pressure mounts, expectations for the finale intensify. If, after all the suspense, the payoff is a water balloon instead of a hand grenade the audience chides itself for its premonitions of excitement. The audience feels cheated and manipulated and turns on the picture.

A single wrong move in the editing can pull the lid off the pressure cooker. If Clint's search has been staged in one long, languorous take, for example, but the editor cuts to a new angle just before Clint's attacker jumps out, the editor telegraphs the punch, dissipating the carefully pumped pressure behind the blow. But if the moment is edited just right—if the new shot isn't just another angle but a menacing view of the attacker revealed when we least expect it—the cut itself becomes the explosive moment, what editors call a "shock cut." We might be on Elm Street, watching the teenager walk through a darkened room (teenagers rarely turn on the lights in these scenes), following her every move, hoping to see her point of view into the shadows—and we suddenly cut to Freddy clicking his steel fingernails. A moment later, he jumps. Which is the bigger payoff, the cut or the jump? Do they reinforce or detract from each other?

There is a contradiction here. We have spent the whole scene building anticipation of the final moment, yet when it comes we want it to be a surprise. In fact, the bigger the surprise the bigger the sense of payoff. Hitchcock often spoke about the difference between suspense and surprise—surprise, he said, is when the characters are having an innocent little chat and suddenly the room blows up; suspense is knowing there is a time bomb ticking under the table. But suspense too depends on the judicious use of surprise. Since suspense depends on the friction between what you know will happen and what you hope will happen, filmmakers have to keep rubbing the two together.

One way to do this is to violate your own carefully created expectations, for the worse. If the audience thinks it knows what is going to happen and suddenly it learns something even worse is in store, the tension level goes up. While the audience hopes for the same result it has even more reason to fear disaster. If the filmmakers establish a time clock, for instance, they can suddenly chop the time left in half—the hurricane changes direction, the timer on the bomb is defective, or Claude Rains, in an expansive mood because his party is going so well, decides he needs more champagne even though half a dozen bottles are left in the cooler.

We can also use our vicarious connection with the actors to gain surprise within suspense. Suppose our teenager has heard a noise; she enters the darkened room to check it out. We know, even if she doesn't yet, that Freddy is lurking somewhere—without that knowledge, we are candidates for Hitchcock's surprise but not his suspense. The teenager is apprehensive. We share her fear, magnified by our knowledge of Freddy's presence, as she checks nooks and crannies for the noise. Then she hears the noise again, whirls—

A

B

C

D

and behind her a cat jumps off the sofa. Her fear changes to relief. At that moment, what we hope (that she'll be safe) coincides with what we know (it was only a cat). Instinctively, our tension drops with hers for just an instant—and that is the instant for Freddy to strike. We have both suspense and surprise.

The surprise effect can come simply from the way a scene is shot. A standard, if cheap, trick in scenes of spatial suspense is to have the victim walk into close-up, look one way, then calmly look the other—and suddenly be attacked from his blind side. Since he just looked in the direction of the attack and didn't see anything, we thought there was nothing to fear. Tension has dropped. Not very credible, but extremely effective—you probably missed it in the gory programmer *The Hills Have Eyes*, and maybe you never saw the demise of the weather forecaster in *The Fog*, but more sophisticated variants cost Harry Dean Stanton and Tom Skerritt their lives and almost scare Sigourney Weaver out of her underwear in *Alien*. This trick works so well because there hasn't been any cut at all. Time and space are unbroken, but danger still strikes when we least expect it.

OPPOSITE PAGE
Wait Until Dark

Consider the indelible climax of *Wait Until Dark*, when the blind Audrey Hepburn breaks away from ruthless killer Alan Arkin. She wounds him and runs to the door—the camera moves close to her as she frantically tries to get out, but the door is chained shut. Now the director, Terence Young, falls back to a wide shot, a tension-dropping move—we are pulling away from Hepburn's desperation to a sort of geographical master angle which seems designed to orient us in preparation for the next scary sequence. Even the scary music (a single menacing chord) fades away. While we're waiting for the master to be over so the director can get on with the scarier stuff, we watch Hepburn give up on the door, come back into the living room—and suddenly Arkin swoops out of the shadows with a knife (and the scare music lashes out again). We know we're at the climax of a very frightening story, but the drop in tension from retreating to the master angle and staying there for an unbroken stretch before Arkin leaps out still lulls us, making his appearance one of the most deliciously terrifying moments in movies.

ACTION

The suspense scene is one long smoldering fuse, but the action scene is a continuous series of explosions. One is all tease, the other all payoff. In the action scene each punch, each leap, each stunt should feel climactic, and the way to make each one a climax is to give each one its own shot.

Here, pace generates energy. The more the scene is broken up into separate bits, each delivered with the maximum kick, the fuller the scene will feel. The lab technician who color-corrected *The Parallax View* told me that the toughest job he ever had was Peckinpah's *Bring Me the Head of Alfredo Garcia*. One twenty-minute reel, all action, had over two hundred and fifty cuts, as many cuts as some ninety-minute films. For Peckinpah, that averages out to a cut every six seconds. Too much, perhaps, for anyone to stand for twenty minutes. In fact, it is paced out—half the cuts come in two brief but bloody action sequences totaling about five minutes of the reel.

If a static scene were chopped up into such tiny bits we would be hopelessly disoriented. Meaning would bleed away in the confusion. But in Peckinpah's film, the cutting may exhaust us but it is never confusing. If cutting rhythms capture the tempo of the action they can heighten the visceral excitement and in that sense give added meaning to the scene.

This kind of editing is cued to movement. When a man throws a punch, we cut to another angle for the impact. When a car races by, the speed and direction of the car (and the camera tracking it) create a rhythm which can be picked up in another shot. Movement is the currency of the visceral world, what the filmmakers must spend to grab and hold their audience. It draws us in and carries us along.

On a big screen, however, movement can be hard to watch, inherently dizzying and confusing for an eye scanning such a large area. The good editor uses the movements of the shots in an orchestrated way, in so-called center-of-interest editing, so movement leads to movement in a choreographed series of images and the action gains a cumulative momentum. The editor is aware of what part of the screen the audience is watching at the last moment of the outgoing shot and tries to match it in the incoming shot so the eye can pick up where it left off.

Since action scenes require so many tiny bits of film, shooting them is a time-consuming and highly technical affair. To cover the same action from different angles, the action must either be repeated again and again or filmed simultaneously by many cameras. The dailies are almost impossible to read. They appear endlessly repetitive, and only an expert eye sifting through the miles of film

can tell whether the crucial snippets will actually work well together. It is not uncommon to have to shoot vital bridging inserts
later—shots that seem trivial but are essential building blocks of
the scene, something like a car's rear wheel churning on gravel or
a hand grabbing a knife—or to turn a shot into its mirror image
optically or to steal something from one place and use it in another.
Producers dread the expensive mistake which would require restag-
ing entire stunts.

Planning, then, is essential. But scenes that require action cutting can never be caught on the written page. Dialogue is irrelevant, and attempts to capture the camera angles and cutting
rhythms with many small paragraphs only lead to choppy hedge-
rows of prose, thickets of words entangling the fast-moving moments of the action scene. The visceral thrill needs pictures.
Writers often retreat into workmanlike notes such as "put director's
chase sequence here," or they hype their action as Bill Goldman
does in his script for *The Princess Bride:* "What we are starting now
is one of the two greatest swordfights in modern movies (the other
one happens later on) . . ." (Goldman can get away with this puf-
fery because his other movies have done half a billion in business.)
Neither of these tactics is particularly helpful for the essential job
of planning out such risky and expensive scenes.

These scenes are worked out in drawings, on storyboards. Storyboards have the advantages of precision and economy—a good
artist can give the filmmakers a sense of exactly what bits of film
they will need to piece the sequence together before they go to the
trouble and expense of shooting anything. The pictures can even
be videotaped to give a rough sense of the sequence, though this
can be misleading because the static pictures will never capture the
flow of movement in the shots. Storyboards give the director the
advantage of a concrete series of images he can show the editor and
the cameraman and the stunt coordinator and the special effects
experts when together they plan the scene, something that can be
pulled apart and minutely critiqued second by second, then used
as a template for the shoot.

The board can begin as a freewheeling conceptual thing, impressionistic swatches of action and movement, but by the time of
shooting we were talking about a highly rendered, precise visual
tool. To work with the director, the storyboard artist has to understand cutting as well as an editor or cameraman, and has to have a
knowledge of optical perspective to depict accurately exactly what

a particular focal-length lens will see. The artist will also need the patience and the ego of a saint (or a screenwriter) because in movie terms the artist's time is cheap and storyboard pictures are looked on by one and all as a kind of visual typewriting, to be endlessly torn up and revised and finally judged only by the finished scene in the movie.

VISCERAL NOISE

The momentum of action and the tension of suspense are peculiarly dependent on the use of sound. Dialogue is irrelevant or distracting, but here sound effects come into their own. Noise triggers the visceral response. Think of what happens in your gut when you suddenly hear your baby cry or a siren wail or vicious barking. Here is the place for the creak of footsteps, the snick of the lock, the metallic snap as a pistol cocks. In suspense, the sounds tend to be exaggeratedly discrete—linear, to stretch out time. In action, they are piled on top of each other to build momentum—an orchestrated cacophony of engines roaring, tires squealing, wind screaming, men groaning, bodies thumping.

OPPOSITE PAGE
Raiders of the Lost Ark
sequence: storyboard and
actual frames

The tone of a movie, its level of abstraction, is set as much by its sounds as its pictures. Fight scenes without the sound of fist on flesh have a curious, insubstantial quality; fight scenes with fist effects that sound like a truck hitting a bridge abutment are ludicrous, or at best highly stylized in the manner of karate pictures from Hong Kong. Multichannel surround-sound, so distracting from a voyeuristic standpoint, packs a wallop here—being enveloped by the sound only adds to the sick roller-coaster thrill of swooping over a Vietnamese village on an air cavalry chopper in *Apocalypse Now*, napalming it to hell.

I will wager you cannot recall that scene without Wagner's "Ride of the Valkyries" ringing in your ears. In fact, it is almost impossible to conceive of a visceral scene without music behind it. In such a subjective world, music creates the emotional space. Yet music in this context is basically a form of emotional sound effect. Structure and melody are beside the point. What matters is an insistent mood and for action an insistent beat. In a suspense sequence, music can mirror the sustained tension of the camera work, or, punctuated with irregular staccato notes, it can add a promise of shock to come; when time is at stake, music can put a ticking metronome under the scene. Modern music of the Philip Glass variety, with its em-

Apocalypse Now

phasis on mesmerizing repetition, makes for especially effective visceral scores.

A strong beat drives an action scene. Fast music can motivate fast cutting as much as the images themselves can, and can stir us with the same visceral thrill. But it is the rare musical composition that does more, that captures the tone of the scene so well that it magnifies its deeper stirrings. Perhaps the most effective visceral score of all is Bernard Herrmann's work in the shower scene in *Psycho*. The score is simplicity itself—a collective violin screech, repeated over and over. Half human shriek of terror, half animal scream of attack, it strikes the perfect emotional chord; its insistent repetition shoves the scene forward like thrusts of the killer's knife. If you want to see what it adds, try watching the scene with the sound turned off.

It is a measure of the difference between the two media that the rules of visceral filmmaking are as good as useless on television. Visceral content—the shoot-out, the porno flick, the creature in *The Fly*—can be affecting on TV, but visceral film techniques are mostly useless. They are developed from the particular relationship between the viewer and the big screen, and, as Arnheim pointed out, watching television is a different physiological process. Because the screen is small the eye doesn't scan it as it does a movie screen (or a real-life scene); instead, it locks in, in a sort of mesmerized parody of the meditative alpha state.

The visceral, the most cinematic part of filmmaking, is most dependent on the full resources of the medium. Center-of-interest cutting is unnecessary on TV because the eye isn't moving; enveloping effects like the big-screen point-of-view shot are unreproducible (the sensation of speed the shots create on TV is the palest reflection of their movie effect). It is impossible to be swept up in a television image—it doesn't extend far enough into the peripheral vision. It can't overpower us. A movie score reproduced through a tinny TV speaker can't have the jolting power of the strings in *Psycho* stabbing us from giant speaker arrays. And if you hear a good stereo system hooked up to a stereo VCR, the startling theaterlike clarity of the sound only points up how puny the image is.

Thus, the better the technician's work—the more he or she uses the full potential of the film medium—the harder it is to translate to TV. Because the eye isn't working as hard watching TV, because it swallows the whole image in a single gulp, extended suspense sequences lose their tension and become tedious. Because the television image has a much narrower contrast range, nuances of light and dark—something flitting in the shadows, for instance—are invisible and extended scenes in darkness are almost unwatchable. For television, films like *Klute* and *The Godfather* must be visually boosted and compressed until they are only a garish overbright simulacrum of the original. TV is film with a myopic visceral eye.

Music videos are revealing in this respect. Pop songs aim at the gut, but with rare exceptions the vapidity of the songs turns rock videos into exercises in form without content, at once the purest type of filmmaking and the most debased. Since the songs are designed for visceral appeal, the video makers naturally turn to the techniques of the visceral film, and they strive mightily to overcome the inherent handicaps of their medium. They labor to impart a sense of gut urgency by ever more frenetic cutting (fast cutting is easier to watch on TV, where the eye doesn't have to scan), by cutting on the beat, dropping out frames and multiplying others, juxtaposing bizarre images, using flashing lights and smoke effects. Because the eye is locked in, because the images flow more freely into the brain without the eye having to work to decipher them, the well-made music video can have a weird, eerie, subliminal impact all its own. Not the gut-grabbing urgency of the visceral but something one more step removed from the outside world, the power of a drug hallucination or a dream.

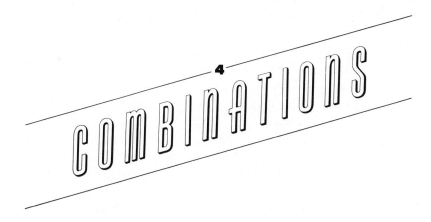

COMBINATIONS

4

THE SURE THING

Movies are an expensive gamble. When producers look to make a movie, they might want perfection but they are asking themselves a much cruder question: how little does this thing need to work? What is the X factor that it must contain that will forgive a thousand blunders?

Producers and studios are always searching for this Holy Grail. The right casting, lots of action, a grand location, a great story—what can they supply that will forgive all else? This question is part fantasy wish fulfillment for anxious producers, but it is forced on them by the hard decisions they have to make about time and money. How should the producer allocate scarce resources: for expensive stars? costly stunts? elaborate sets? There is only so much to go around, and this initial commitment might well be the single most critical step in making a movie.

Directors, for their part, live in the same imperfect world and are often forced to take on less than ideal material. The good ones are guided by a passion—yes, a piece might have faults, they tell themselves, but it has some strong element that possesses them. Sometimes it's a clever premise, more often a compelling relationship or a vivid character, perhaps a combination of actors that promises to be exciting. If the strengths of the material are suffi-

OPPOSITE PAGE
TOP: *The Fly II*, MIDDLE: *Ninotchka*, BOTTOM: *2001: A Space Odyssey*

ciently appealing, the director will take it on hoping to find a way around the weaknesses.

So both producer and director are pressed to make clear-cut decisions about where to gamble their movie, pushing it more into one of the three worlds I've described—toward the rich voyeuristic pleasures of spectacle and story, the profound emotional rewards of the vicarious experience, the gut thrills of the visceral.

If these worlds are so powerful, is any one of them a formula for success all by itself? They are all tempting, and they've all been tried. But even executed to perfection, a film that lives in just one of the three worlds can never be more than an interesting failure. Each of the three points of view, all by itself, is ultimately self-defeating.

A purely voyeuristic film might seem to have the most potential. What can be more fun than chasing a good story through a fresh new world? Yet while the voyeuristic experience by itself can sustain an Eames short, at theatrical length even the most lavishly mounted, ingeniously worked out story that doesn't engage us emotionally will be a cold and forbidding two hours. We may admire its beauty and its cleverness, but we will not be moved by it. The films whose voyeuristic elements we never forget, films like *The Last Emperor*, *The Guns of Navarone*, *Topkapi*, and *Star Wars*, offer much more.

A vicarious film gives us cathartic insight into human nature and the human condition, which is the movies' real claim to higher meaning. In a good vicarious film we aren't just touched, we are profoundly shaken. If you have a great star in a great role what more can you need? And yet a film that is all vicarious moments is a film that stresses character at the expense of story and place; it is a film of great performances but deadeningly static, disturbingly amorphous content. The stuff of a Proustian novel, perhaps, but not the stuff of Hollywood box office, not films with indelible characters like *The Hustler*, *East of Eden*, and *On the Waterfront*.

The visceral world is big box office. Critics may hate to admit it, but hot visceral thrills pack the theaters. They're what movies do best and what Hollywood producers feel most comfortable pushing. Yet as producers are constantly rediscovering, action alone won't do the job—even on their own terms the purest visceral films need more. While they hit us directly and hit us hard, we rapidly build up a tolerance for their assaults. As in *1941*, Spielberg's only flop, twice as much comes off as half as effective. Audiences need to be

paced, and they need charismatic actors in arresting roles to identify with, stories to credibly motivate the thrills. The visceral impact
of films like *Psycho*, *Rambo*, *The Fly* and *Aliens* depends on what
else they offer.

3-D showed what happens when overeager producers come
down too hard on the side of the visceral. Amid all the hoopla when
it first came out, there was speculation that 3-D might become as
much a part of the movie idiom as sound or color or the wide screen
—after all, it brings the screen experience one step closer to life.

Limitations of the technology as much as assured its failure, but
it was not a passing mourned by filmmakers. Like Imax, 3-D was
more constricting than liberating. Other values in the film paled
beside the gimmick; we sat there waiting for the yo-yo or the flaming
arrows to part our hair. Lighting and camera placement were dic-
tated by the need for maximum 3-D effect, and the way 3-D destroyed the plane of the screen, beauties of composition were a
thing of the past. 3-D created such a rigorous geometric space that
the camera could not move freely; as in Imax, switching angles
really did make viewers feel they were lurching about in space.
When we saw an over-the-shoulder shot, the dark fuzzy mass
loomed menacingly in the foreground, when we saw a close-up
there was no visual cue for the 3-D effect so the scene seemed to
flatten out.

Even the most sophisticated filmmakers were at the mercy of the
third dimension—it is no accident that *Dial M for Murder*, Hitchcock's attempt at 3-D, is the most ploddingly shot of all his films.
3-D was actually a step backward, weakening the mix, impoverish-
ing the film experience by overbalancing it toward the visceral and
ultimately trivializing even that.

Rambo isn't *Sophie's Choice*. The mix can vary, but there must
be a mix to make the movie work. Take our mountain climber
working his way up Half Dome without a rope. Watching him gives
me a visceral thrill—I'm not sharing his feelings, I'm thinking he
has to be crazy to be up there. Yet vicariously watching his cool
demeanor adds to my gut thrill; watching a mountain goat would
be a kick, but this is a bigger kick. This is a person I can admire. I
can wonder at his calm skill. If in addition there is a sound story
reason for him to be climbing without a rope—if he'd lost the rope
or if seconds were a matter of life and death and he couldn't spare
the time to tie on—the gut thrill intensifies even more. Even por-
traying the climber in a grand voyeuristic vista, as a mere pink

pebble on the mountain, can give the scene more impact. From that perspective the climber fuses with the mountain, he becomes an atom in the macrocosm.

Producers acknowledge the mix when they tell directors that action films need star presence. Eastwood in a subpar action script like *The Dead Pool* will draw crowds; that's why he gets such a hefty salary. The action, our thrills, are there without him. What is the extra satisfaction he affords?

The same thing Marlon Brando brings to *One-Eyed Jacks*. When Karl Malden whips Brando and smashes his gun hand, the pain is visceral—Brando is only a conduit for our own sensation. But the pain is only half the equation. Yes, it gives us a kick, perhaps more of a kick than we would like to admit, but the visceral jolt arouses other emotions in us—rage, revenge. Emotions no one embodies like Brando. Brando's bravery, his stoicism, his strength of will give us tremendous vicarious satisfaction. We feel them because Brando is Brando, charismatic, sensitive, and strong. Without Brando, the scene is a squalid visceral scene of torture; with Brando, it is a rousing vicarious scene of bravery triumphant in defeat. The visceral is what kicks the vicarious into gear, and the vicarious is what gives us permission to indulge our visceral pleasures.

THE VISCERAL:
PSYCHO

The shower scene in *Psycho* is generally accepted as one of the scariest moments in movies. Yet much of the visceral shock of the shower scene comes from the skillful way Hitchcock plays it off against the vicarious and the voyeuristic.

In the first place, the scene shocks because it is so completely unexpected: we are caught up in a different tale entirely, a tale of love and embezzlement, not murder, when the killer leaps out and cuts down the last person we would expect to be his victim, the star of the movie. This is Hitchcock's surprise, not his suspense. This is a triumph of story, of the voyeur's eye—a story carefully plotted so that nothing preceding the scene makes us suspect an attack, though in retrospect it makes perfect sense.

The sequence begins on a voyeuristic note—literally. Through a hidden peephole Tony Perkins watches Janet Leigh take off her clothes. There is an element of titillation in this, but basically we're in the world of story. The next thing we see, which we don't think Perkins sees, is Leigh creating a clue (working some figures about

OPPOSITE PAGE
One-Eyed Jacks

OVERLEAF
One frame from every cut of the shower sequence in *Psycho* (except for 7–7a, where the camera moves in before the shower curtain is pulled aside to reveal the killer). Frames 8–38 take just 22 seconds of screen time.

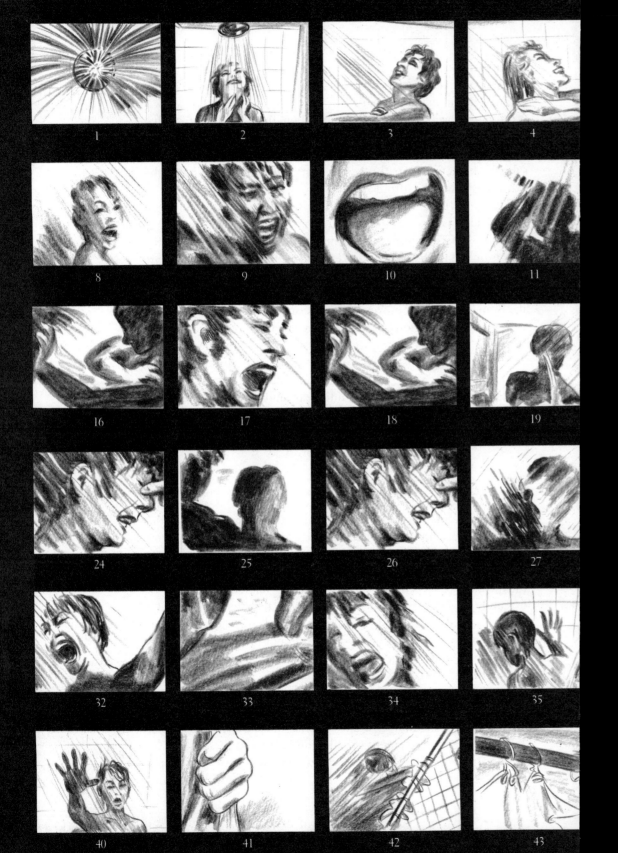

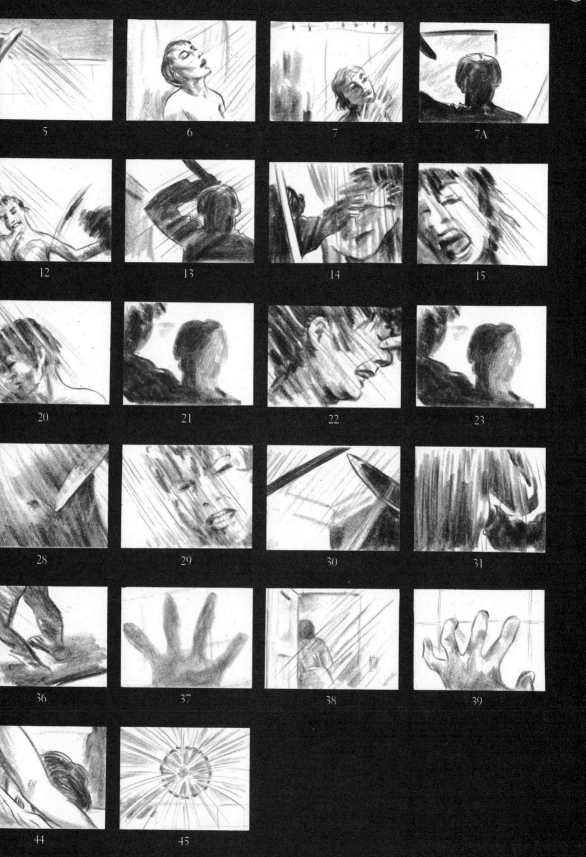

her stolen money) and then carefully destroying it by flushing it down the toilet. This is given enough attention that we feel it is bound to matter later (it does). Leigh then steps into the shower and in an extended sequence unwraps the soap, turns on the water, and lathers herself. We linger on her showering—again Hitchcock hints at titillation (this is a film about sexual perversion after all, and if our own sap is rising it will give the action more personal bite), but we're also wondering whether there isn't some story point involved. Is Perkins watching her again? Perhaps this time she will discover him.

Indistinctly, through the shower curtain, we see the bathroom door open. Our plot musings end abruptly—this must be Perkins, entering to make a pass at Leigh. Then the curtain is pulled aside —and it isn't Perkins, it's a woman, and she's holding a knife.

Suddenly, the scene is wrenched into the visceral. The knife comes down, the violins scream, we see thirty-one images in the next twenty-two seconds, picture cuts cued to the slashing knife. We see the knife come down, then we see Leigh's screaming face —a vicarious image, as we feel her fear—then we're close on her screaming mouth, so large on the screen we're almost inside it— not a vicarious image, not a way to share her emotions but to trigger our own. We see the knife come down, we see her try to hold it off, three times more we see the knife come down and then we see her face as she is stabbed, we see the knife come down and we see it flash past her naked torso, we see the knife come down and in a looser single we see her sink into a stupor. We see the killer leave.

Notice that while this is a visceral scene par excellence, Hitchcock spices the visceral with vicarious moments of Leigh's shock and fear as counterpoint to the mayhem. We are feeling the moment as our own—but we are also seeing it through her eyes.

Not through the eyes of the killer. Hitchcock shrouds the killer in darkness, though in the actual lighting of the bathroom "she" should be as brightly light as her victim. The shots intercutting the two ricochet between an anonymous shadow plunging a dark knife and flashes of Leigh's face in a classic empathic close-up, asking us to share her shock and pain.

We feel, as we watch, that this is entirely appropriate—she is the star, and the way the scene is constructed, with her is exactly where we want to be. But it also neatly solves a nasty story problem since seeing the killer distinctly would telegraph the rest of the movie. It is a measure of Hitchcock's brilliance that he has found a way of shooting the visceral scene which feels so right, which captures so precisely our imagined terrors of attack, that we accept the shrouded killer as a trick of visceral perception rather than a manipulation to serve his story.

The brutal scene leaves us stunned. Hitchcock has rushed us through the visceral moment; now he must give us time to absorb what has happened. But Janet Leigh is dead, and while her corpse can shock, she can no longer serve as a vicarious vehicle. How to drive home our horror?

When Henry Fonda holds his newborn son in *Drums Along the Mohawk*, John Ford puts a lump in our throats by showing him to us through the eyes of his loving wife. Hitchcock uses the same technique here: he brings in another character, in this case Perkins, whose reactions give us permission to let out all our emotional stops. But this works both ways for Hitchcock (as so many things do). Since we already feel the death so strongly, Perkins' show of pain and disgust gains him our sympathy too.

Hitchcock then pushes Perkins one step further. He is not only a young man of feeling but he is burdened with a terrible nightmare of a family secret, and he doesn't crumple under the strain. Ever the dutiful son, he now mops up the mayhem to protect his "mother" (though the poor fellow is in such a state of shock he never takes off his suit jacket for the messy work). Perkins not only earns our sympathy by sharing our horror, he earns our respect for his stoic bravery and resourcefulness. It is hard to remember the first release of the film, when we didn't know Perkins himself was the killer, but such is the strength of the sequence that even after we know the truth our heart goes out to poor Norman Bates.

Finally, Perkins pushes Leigh's car into the swamp with her body in the trunk. For a few agonizing moments the car won't sink. We see the panic and desperation on Perkins' face; in an astonishing switch, we find ourselves actually rooting for the car to disappear. Hitchcock has turned us so far around that five minutes after we've seen his star brutally murdered he has us cheering for a man to hide her body. Perkins may have his emotional problems, Hitchcock is saying, but he is your hero now. He is your vicarious connection to this film.

This vicarious sleight of hand, more than the shower sequence, is the true tour de force of *Psycho*. It is unique in Hollywood films —in what other movie does the star die halfway through? And here the murderer even becomes the protagonist. Yet we accept the switch without a murmur because we have been softened up so effectively by the visceral pyrotechnics of the shower sequence.

A B C

D E F

Hitchcock begins in a voyeuristic vein, using our involvement in a story twist to set up his big visceral scene; that scene, in turn, sets up the crucial vicarious moment in the film.

Hitchcock, more than any other director, shifts effortlessly among the different worlds, relishing the heat he generates from their friction. He moves with daring and an almost schoolboy pleasure in shock, but it's a dangerous game. Failure is calamitous. In Truffaut's *Hitchcock*, the director blames the collapse of his film *Sabotage* on his decision to have a little boy carry a bomb through London:

> I made a serious mistake in having the little boy carry the bomb. A character who unknowingly carries a bomb around as if it were an ordinary package is bound to work up great suspense in the audience. The boy was involved in a situation that got him too much sympathy from the audience, so that when the bomb exploded and he was killed, the public was resentful.

OPPOSITE PAGE
Psycho

Here, vicarious feeling for the boy undermined the visceral thrill of suspense. But such mistakes are the price of Hitchcock's willingness to take the risk. When he succeeds, his films take on a peculiar resonant power—they are pulpy, juicy, crowd-pleasing thrillers and also something deeper, more disturbing, more profound.

THE VICARIOUS:
SOPHIE'S CHOICE

Sophie's Choice is as pure an example of a vicarious film as has emerged from Hollywood in years. Highly praised when it came out —Meryl Streep won the Oscar for best actress and Alan Pakula, the writer, director, and producer, was nominated for best screenplay —it was nonetheless attacked by some critics as "literary" and did only respectably at the box office. Complex, insightful, at times profoundly moving, it was more a wrenching emotional exploration of hope and despair than an entertainment, and audiences responded by choosing entertainment. Yet few would dispute that it succeeds impressively on its own terms.

Potential backers were concerned that because of the shape of the tale, adapting the Styron novel was a hopeless task. It is a tangled, relatively inert love story, and a large chunk of the last half occurs in a concentration-camp flashback at Auschwitz. Yet Pakula has said that the novel's shape was for him one of its chief attractions.

While the action might not progress in a conventional story sequence, there is a motor to the plot of a more vicarious sort. The novel consists of a series of revelations about two characters, Nathan and Sophie, from the point of view of a third, Stingo. It is constructed as a successive peeling back of their layers as Stingo learns more about them. At each moment we think we know the two lovers, only to discover a moment later that we didn't know them at all. Charming, witty Nathan becomes a jealous monster, then contrite charmer again—and then we realize he's insane and everything we've accepted about him is pure invention. Beautiful Sophie at first entrances Stingo as the ultimately desirable woman; then she becomes a victim of Nathan's rage, someone for Stingo to protect and maybe even make his own; finally, he learns she is beyond saving.

The book may be short on story (except for the flashbacks), but the character revelations are so skillfully orchestrated that we are propelled along by our curiosity about human nature, our vicarious desire to see what makes people tick, until we're finally shown the awful moment in Auschwitz when Sophie is forced to choose which of her children will live and which will die. And then we're back in the present for the inevitable, almost anticlimactic suicide of Nathan and Sophie.

Sophie's awful choice is a brilliant invention by Styron. In a single story beat, a single dramatic moment, he apotheosizes the terrible toll exacted by the Holocaust on the living. After that moment we know the appalling guilt that haunts Sophie, and we know that as fervently as she embraces life, she must ultimately choose death.

Sophie's moment of choice is exceptional in another way, too—it is the rare example of a potent literary idea that is also supremely cinematic. On film, Pakula extracts its unique, wrenching power.

After a brief silent interlude showing Sophie clutching her children in a cattle car, we see Sophie's son in close-up, then Sophie and her daughter, waiting nervously on the Auschwitz platform. Suddenly we jump to the panoramic: Pakula establishes the mood of his scene with two grim, sweeping shots of the concentration-camp rail yards. These are striking not only for their fine execution but because there are so few big shots in the film; Pakula the producer has decided to spend the film's tight budget on vicarious concerns. But here he pulls out all the stops. In broad, floating shots we glide over squalid masses of prisoners herded into line by Nazi guards, finally at the tag end of a camera move alighting on Sophie and her children.

From the grand to the claustrophobic—a German officer strides into tight close-up, says a few words to Sophie, and moves on. Sophie, trying to save herself, calls after him. She believes in Christ, she says. The Nazi turns back to face her, and the look in his eyes tells Sophie that appealing to this man was a dreadful mistake. Quoting Scripture ("Did he not say, 'Suffer the little children to come unto me?' "), he forces her to make her choice.

The exchange is contained in a back-and-forth series of tight, almost cramped over-the-shoulder shots. These shots are the largest heads in the film (if not here, where?), but the actor we're watching is crowded by the other one, dark in the foreground, and Sophie's angle has her little daughter stirring on the fringes. "Choose," he says. "I cannot, I cannot," she replies. The moments are spare, tense, beautifully acted. Her anguish is our own.

Finally, the Nazi loses patience and calls for soldiers to take away both children. Now the metronomic back-and-forth shift between the two close-ups is ruptured by a brief, sharp sequence: five quick cuts of the soldiers coming, Sophie clutching the boy ("Take the baby, take my little girl"), confusion of movement as they grab the girl away. The child shrieks and shrieks, like the violins in *Psycho*; now Sophie is left alone in the frame watching her child disappear in the distance. Though we certainly feel the child's anguish, Pakula doesn't show her in close-up but only from Sophie's point of view. He wants to keep our emotional bonds firmly attached to Sophie.

This superbly acted scene is as powerful as any in movies. More than life and death is at stake here. We are witness to the destruction of a soul. And because the scene is so sublimely realized, so deeply understood by the director, so deeply felt by the actress, the vicarious bonds tear out a piece of our souls too. The scene has the profoundly disturbing power of recurring nightmare.

Even in this, the classic vicarious scene, Pakula realized that the crucial moment must have a visceral edge to it. We must not only feel the crisis through Sophie (powerful though that is), we must also feel it directly, as if it were happening to us, as if the Nazis weren't only taking away Sophie's child but *our* child. He edited the moment of truth, when the guards take the little girl, as a visceral action scene—many quick cuts cued by movement, in which we

1.
You may keep one
of your children.

2.

3.
I can't choose!
I can't choose!

4.
Choose! Or I'll send them
both over there!

5.
Don't make me choose!
I can't!

6.
Shut up! Enough!

7.
—I'll send them both over there!
—I can't choose!

8.
Take *both* children away!

9.
Move!

10.
Take my little girl!

11.

12.
Take my baby!

13.

14.

15.

16.

don't even see Sophie's face clearly—and scored it with the girl's screams. Deft cutting slides the scene into the visceral and out again. Pakula never descends into cheap thrills, but the visceral shivers are there in the service of Meryl Streep's superb performance, driving it like a dagger into our heart.

A gauge of Pakula's success here is the letdown of the subsequent scene, when after Sophie's ghastly confession she and Stingo make love. We hear Stingo's voice telling us:

> I was twenty-two, and a virgin, and was clasping in my arms at last the goddess of my unending fantasies. My lust was inexhaustible. Sophie's lust was both a plunge into carnal oblivion and a flight from memory and grief. More than that, I now see, it was a frantic and orgiastic attempt to beat back death.

Instead of the scene of orgiastic lust Stingo describes, Pakula gives us a restrained, melancholic union, discreetly observed. Pakula holds back, and the moment suffers for it. There is no visceral component, no lust igniting us to color our perception of their lovemaking; the extra emotional juice of guilty grief transmuted into carnal passion isn't there. Hitchcock might have chosen a more lurid color, and the raw, crude passion of the moment would have deepened, not degraded, the lovers' joining.

Is Sophie's choice as terrifying to someone with no children? Knowing for myself the intense pleasure and pain of parental love I can't imagine it is. (My wife, who had given birth to our first child a few months before she saw the film, wept uncontrollably.) Yet one certainly doesn't have to be a parent to be profoundly affected by the scene. We all secretly fear that our souls will be crushed, and only a stone could be witness to Streep's luminous performance and not share the desperate finality of the moment.

In any vicarious scene there is an exchange of emotions. Here we simultaneously feel Sophie's and project our own, and it is tempting to say that we can only feel her emotion because we identify it with something we have felt ourselves. On the most subterranean level, on the level of infantile fears and wishes, that must be true. Yet I have never had anything approaching Sophie's experience. What the scene touches is not my own trivial version of the moment—when I've had to choose which child to play with, my son or my daughter, or when I've lost one of them briefly in a supermarket. It touches fears of mine which have never been realized, my darkest fears of what could happen to them, my shamefully selfish fears of what their loss would do to me.

Without those fears, how could I be touched by the scene? There is a curious contradiction in our emotional connection to movies. We pay good money for the chance to project our own emotions into situations we've never experienced, but if the situations are genuinely new to us our emotions can't take hold. We lose our cathartic pleasure.

We twist a scene to fit our own emotional makeup. Ingrid Bergman has a star's power over me. I respond to her emotional beacon. I feel what she feels, with pleasure at the privilege. But when I watch a love scene between Cary Grant and Ingrid Bergman I must watch it differently than my wife does. I'm rooting for Grant. For a few moments, I'm lucky enough to share Grant's way with women. I feel the characters' mutual attraction, but I'm also fantasizing about Bergman looking into my eyes that way. Here again the two-shot proves its advantages over the single—if both lovers are in the frame we can choose which one to identify with, and my wife and I can each watch the scene happily from our different points of view.

This emotional provincialism may explain the signal lack of popular success of films about homosexuality. I can watch the actors vicariously, empathize with them, but I hold back from projecting my own emotions into the situation. I'm afraid to blur the distinction between what I feel for a woman and what the homosexual character feels for another man.

When a nude woman in a heterosexual love scene triggers my visceral instincts, I'm drawn in; when a nude man triggers my visceral instincts in a homosexual love scene, I draw away in self-defense. If, in spite of my reluctance, the film really works and pulls at my visceral chords, my buried homosexual side, I feel profoundly threatened and shut myself off completely in self-protection. It is either that or conversion, and powerful as the film experience is it's not about to change my sexual orientation. Homosexuality is not an impossible theme, but works aimed at a heterosexual audience have to take this double bind into account. It's a tough knot to cut through.

At the other end of the scale, if people cannot distinguish between their own lives and life on the screen, the emotional distance between viewer and subject collapses. The vicarious and the visceral fuse to generate the Hinckley effect, where the viewer becomes so enmeshed in the emotions on the screen that he tries to realize them in life, even if it means trying to assassinate a president.

THE VOYEURISTIC:
2001 AND
ALL THE PRESIDENT'S MEN

The voyeuristic world is where movies began. Before anyone thought that film could portray character, before the great innovators of the twenties had invented montage and tapped the visceral power of film editing, films were traveling tent shows that first promised exotic sights mysteriously brought to life, then the melodrama of a simple story. As film evolved, the emphasis shifted; now it is a common complaint that film-school Hollywood directors, raised on movies rather than plays and novels, are so taken with movie magic, with gut effects and star turns, that they've sacrificed the pleasures of place and story, thinking that movies don't need them anymore.

American viewers, these directors argue, are so visually sophisticated these days, so trained by TV commercials to follow lightning montage, that their films must follow a less literal, more allusive logic. These filmmakers say they can't afford to slow down, to take the time to create a place, to let a story unfold at its own rhythm; they might even say it's a waste of effort.

2001: A Space Odyssey proves that the pleasures of the tent show still pack a wallop. From the viewpoint of normal Hollywood storytelling it's a very strange film indeed. It is not held together by character (the "hero" doesn't appear until fifty-one minutes into the film) or location, or plot in the normal sense of the word. It is four distinct films, connected only by the presence of an extraterrestrial black monolith: first, a sixteen-minute film of ape-men touching the monolith and discovering the first tool; then, a thirty-five-minute film of a bureaucrat in the twenty-first century managing the rediscovery of the monolith; then, an hourlong film of an astronaut outwitting his computer on the way to explore the monolith's source on Jupiter; and finally, a half-hour trip-out to "Jupiter and beyond the infinite."

The segments are loosely clustered around the theme of man's evolution—where we came from and where we are going and the

2001: A Space Odyssey

light that sheds on what we are. But they're really held together by an attitude of the filmmaker. This is a tale told from a distance. The characters have a bland, remote quality (it's no accident that the only memorable personality in the movie is a computer). The story shuns false drama. Instead of hyping his tale, director Stanley Kubrick moves with supreme confidence in his material, going to great pains to make what happens in his scenes feel completely mundane. He is banking on the voyeur's impulse. "I am taking you someplace no one has ever been before," he is saying, "and if you're not interested, that's your problem."

The film opens with panoramic views of earth at the "Dawn of Man." Not one or two views for ten or twenty seconds as we would normally expect, but twelve different epic vistas unfold for a minute and forty seconds of screen time before we see any sign of life at all. Later, when we first cut to the year 2001, we spend more than five minutes floating through space before we have any scenes of plot or character; then we spend two minutes watching Dr. Floyd clear immigration and two minutes watching him place a long-distance call of no particular importance. Once Dr. Floyd (who soon disappears completely from our story) leaves the space station, we spend three minutes watching Pan Am stewardesses serving dinner in zero gravity and four minutes and twenty seconds, fully sixteen extremely complicated composite shots, watching the Pan Am space liner land on the moon. None of this has any story content, character subtext, or suspense to keep us watching. And it's all entrancing.

How does Kubrick get away with it? By creating worlds so richly envisioned and minutely realized that they have their own mesmerizing fascination. The movie came out in 1968, when drugs were supposed to be good for you, and it was known as the ultimate movie "trip." But even now it's still a trip: we are time travelers. This *is* the future. The science, past and future, hasn't dated; the stewardesses have a sixties look about them, but otherwise the world of *2001* seems as credible now as when it was first invented. It is an enduring achievement of the cinematic imagination.

Kubrick's film, of course, is not purely spectacle. The errant computer HAL is such a vivid invention that he created a new character cliché. To soften us up for his climax, Kubrick developed the visceral techniques of slit-scan photography, as close as anyone has come to the distilled sensation of pure speed. But this is not a film of gut thrills or a character film. It is a film, perhaps the ultimate film, of voyeuristic spectacle.

It is a voyeuristic film, but not a plotty film. It was based not on a novel but on Arthur Clarke's brief short story, "The Sentinel." What story there is is expertly told, but by normal standards the piece is fragmented and patchy, and moment to moment very little happens (we're spending all that screen time watching space hostesses serve dinner). Only in the second hour, when Keir Dullea and his partner match wits with HAL, is there what might normally be called clever plotting—HAL goes bad and the astronauts conspire against him until HAL reads their lips and double-crosses them, locking Dullea out of the ship; then Dullea must reenter without his helmet so he blows the hatch. The plotting certainly doesn't make or break the movie. For the most part, Kubrick keeps the pages turning simply by showing us one amazing sight after another.

Plot and spectacle seem poles apart: one is entirely movement, and in the other nothing happens at all. But like action and suspense, they are two sides of the same mental coin. Both depend on obsessive love of detail, both concern objective facts rather than subtleties of character, both are subjected to tests of logic and credibility.

Strictly speaking, plot and story are not the same thing. In normal usage the words are interchanged, but, technically, plot is that part of the story that isn't driven by our empathic interest in character—the voyeuristic part as opposed to the vicarious part. In

Lillian Hellman's words, story is what the characters want to do and plot is what the writer wants the characters to do. In *2001*, the astronauts talk secretly about their distrust of HAL; the writer has them do this where HAL can read their lips. Dullea leaves the ship to retrieve his friend; the writer makes him forget his helmet. HAL locks him out of the ship; the writer gives Dullea's space dinghy an escape hatch with explosive bolts that just fits the manual hatch on the mother ship so he can blow himself inside.

Taken a step further, the plot is also the way the writer structures the character part, the story. The story of *Citizen Kane* is Kane's lifelong attempt to get love without ever giving it; the plot is the reporter's search for Rosebud and the way the writer, Herman Mankiewicz, uses it to arrange and reveal Kane's history. (The reporter himself is a plot invention: bland, impassive, as close to characterless as a character can credibly be.) The story of *The Maltese Falcon* concerns the pursuit of the film's many characters for the jewel-encrusted bird and all the murder and chicanery that entails, including the seductive high jinks of Mary Astor. The plot is Bogart's quest (and ours) to make sense of the events—what is revealed when, to whom. This is laid out in a sequence to suit the needs of the writer: we think Bogart is stuck with the job of consoling his murdered partner's widow, for instance, only to see her fall

The Maltese Falcon

into his arms like a lover. Then and only then do we learn they're having an affair.

Well done, as in *Citizen Kane* and *The Maltese Falcon*, there is such a confluence of plot and story that it's impossible to imagine one without the other, but plot is a vital element in its own right. It is the essence of the mystery film. It keeps viewers on the edge of their seats by challenging them to piece together the story themselves from carefully presented fragments. It relies on the viewers' concentration, intelligence, and perception to involve them in the tale. This has always been risky business.

Few films these days can match the tight twists of a good forties detective tale. But how many films even back then were as well plotted as *The Maltese Falcon*? Even in the heyday of the detective film, the bread and butter of plotting, exposition (telling why what happened happened), was viewed with suspicion. As Raymond Chandler noted in *Raymond Chandler Speaking* in 1949:

> . . . the best solution is the Hollywood rule: "no exposition except under heat, and break it up at that." (This means that an explanation must always be an accompaniment to some kind of action, and that it must be given in short doses rather than all at once.)

Audiences want a clever solution, but they want it as a flash of insight, not a game of chess. Chess is hard to follow on film. Nowadays it is the rare producer who will take a chance on a movie just because the plot is well worked out. Taking the plunge demands a precarious faith in the intelligence and curiosity of audiences, a faith rare among purveyors of mass entertainment.

Yet the pleasures of a well-plotted story are real nonetheless, and once in a while a script comes along that sorely tests the producer's resolve. *All the President's Men* was a case in point. On the face of it, it seemed the perfect voyeuristic project: adapting a best-selling book about the biggest detective story in American history, an intricate tale of informers, clues, and double-cross in which two young unknowns, by sheer dint of wits and persistence, bring down the most powerful man in the world. It wasn't only a good story, it was even true. (Truth helps a story in Hollywood; to producers, at least, it means people are more likely to want to watch it and more apt to accept what they see.)

Robert Redford got an early look at the manuscript and saw its potential. He envisaged a small, documentary-style film with unknowns in the leads, but when he approached Warner Brothers, with whom he had his production deal, they were less than enthusiastic. They commissioned market research, which told them not to make the film. People were fed up with Watergate, they were told, and by the time the movie came out a good year later America would with great relief be on to other things. Robert Redford being Robert Redford, however, Warner Brothers agreed to make the movie—but only if he would star in it and only then if they could match him with a star of equal magnitude. That would at least guarantee them a strong opening weekend. (As producer Larry Gordon said in a different context, "A star is someone who can open shit.") So Redford lined up Dustin Hoffman and then brought in Alan Pakula, as much for his East Coast dress and manners, I was told, as for his directorial instincts. Redford needed a man with whom the Washington *Post* and the political potentates would feel comfortable.

Pakula's take on the movie was radically different from Redford's. Even though he was to star, Redford was still thinking of it as a gritty, realistic drama. Hoffman was as much a character actor as a star anyway, and Redford wanted to dye his hair and play the movie as a slice of life. Pakula talked him out of it.

Pakula pointed out that star presence wasn't something to hide. The movie needed stars. There was, after all, no secret about the outcome so there was no story advantage to anonymous leads, and the plot was so complicated that they couldn't afford to waste time on character exposition. I'm told he quoted Hitchcock's dictum that casting a star saves twenty minutes of character development since the audience is already on the star's side from the beginning and doesn't need to be won over. (Hitchcock went further, noting in Truffaut's book that "whenever the hero isn't portrayed by a star, the whole picture suffers, because audiences are far less concerned about the predicament of a character who's played by someone they don't know.") If *All the President's Men* was to become a Hollywood extravaganza, so be it.

While Pakula realized that credibility was crucial to the success of the film, he also saw that the film would never be a documentary. Pakula wanted a script with the ring of truth, sets and costumes of absolute accuracy, intensely natural performances—and all the technical gloss of the glitziest extravaganza. It was a Hollywood movie, a chance to watch movie stars on the big screen, and in order to hold the audience through the complex story he would need all the star power and all the cinematic style he could muster.

All the President's Men

Audiences would know it was real; how could Pakula keep them from saying, "Okay, it's real, so what?"

He had to play his tune in perfect pitch. The craft had to pump up the movie, but the movie could never feel inflated. Redford was right when he said that the film must be credible above all; Pakula took the gamble that he could have the best of both worlds, that he could generate sufficient reality in the writing and sets and performances to afford to jack up the drama by shooting it in high style and casting as two unknown reporters the biggest stars in Hollywood. It was, after all, only a movie.

This conflict over the look of the film reflected a fundamental confusion about the theme. What was the movie about? This is never as easy a question to answer while you're making a movie as it is when you view the finished film. In fact, the process of making a movie, from first draft to rewrites, to finding a director and more rewrites, to casting, to budgeting and scheduling and shooting and editing and scoring and even planning the ad campaign and the release pattern can be thought of as a process of closing in on what the movie is about. If the filmmakers are at cross-purposes, they can bounce around in the oddest ways—the film can carom from a trenchant social commentary to a love story to a music video, as in the case of *Flashdance*, but if everyone pulls in the same direction with luck they will generate a series of successive approximations, honing in on what the film was really about all along.

The filmmakers who made *Cocoon*, for example, the warmly received film about aliens who land at a Florida retirement home, didn't realize that their movie was really about the old people until they were deep into postproduction. "Featuring [the old people] as prominently as we did was something that happened in the editing process," says Lili Zanuck, coproducer of the film. "In the screenplay," she says diplomatically,

> they were very carefully balanced against the other elements. In fact, the fear that the film wouldn't work for an audience was so strong that [20th Century-Fox] dictated that members of our older cast were not to have their pictures taken for publicity reasons without a member of the young cast. And the poster was just the hardest thing to come up with because we couldn't use the older cast members in it at all.

From the beginning, there was a wide range of ideas of what *All the President's Men* was really about, which caused considerable nervousness and uncertainty. There was studio concern that it might be a "political" movie, for which read painfully controversial and death at the box office. Surely the film had to give a feel for what makes our system work and what pushes it out of whack or the story wouldn't make any sense. But did that mean the movie was actually about the abuse of power in high places and the responsibility of a free press to protect democracy from corruption by the likes of Nixon? This was dangerous stuff from a studio point of view since they couldn't afford to alienate the legions of loyal Republicans, but it was also what gave the story larger meaning. When I ran the movie for members of the film community in India, where Indira Gandhi had a few years before declared a state of emergency and attempted to muzzle the press, they saw it as a paean to the fourth estate.

Or was it really America's greatest detective story? Unfortunately, while this detective work may have been for high stakes, it left a lot to be desired from the detective writer's point of view. It was a story whose action was words, and ten-dollar words at that, a hopelessly tangled web ensnarling a vast array of characters who did nothing but talk about complex things done by other people before the movie even started, things we never see on screen. Worse yet, there were no dead bodies—not even a thrown punch or a drawn gun. The best the story could summon of Chandler's visceral "smell of fear" was a paranoia of the most generalized sort.

Was it a kind of buddy picture, "Butch and Sundance bring down the government?" Certainly the casting would point in this direction, and it was no accident that William Goldman, who wrote *Butch Cassidy and the Sundance Kid*, was chosen as the screenwriter. Meticulous Woodward and impulsive Bernstein do have an engaging odd-couple quality, but as a character story the script was exceptionally thin. We see no particular growth in our characters. We see not a single scene of their private lives. We meet not a single person they really care about, no wife or lover or child or parent. In this respect the script defied conventional Hollywood wisdom, and in fact at Hoffman's urging a scene was shot between Bernstein and his wife. It was one of the first to end up on the floor. And yet without the odd-couple charm of Redford and Hoffman this would be a very difficult movie to watch.

In a sense everyone was right. The film had to involve all these elements. Yet they still weren't enough. Complex as a film is, one theme must dominate and pull it together. This film is about something, but not what I thought it was about at the time, and not what I heard anyone else articulate until the movie was almost in release. It is an odd, out-of-the-way theme, certainly not one producers would set out to make into a big-budget movie. Though Redford or Pakula may disagree, I think what it was really about emerged only during the editing. (As associate producer I was on the set for every day of shooting and in the editing room whenever the director was there.)

All the President's Men is about why people talk to the press or, in larger terms, the human need to unburden oneself. The press, unlike the priesthood, offers no absolution. Even the anonymous informant runs enormous risks—to his job, his reputation, even his freedom. Why talk?

To the movie's credit, nobody in it asks this question. Nobody discusses his motives, and rightly, for the characters' behavior is not something to be debated but to be watched. *All the President's Men*, like most detective movies, can be thought of as a series of confrontations in which the hero uses information to pry out more information. But this movie uses that form in a new way. In something like *The Maltese Falcon*, the detective squeezes information out of people by exploiting the usual combinations of baser human motives—greed, jealousy, fear, anger, desire. Sam Spade twists people's emotions to get at the truth, and people twist Spade's in return, to use him for their own purposes or to get him off the case.

The fun of the scenes lies in the clash of wills and the way emotions are manipulated to get more new information.

In *All the President's Men* it is not nearly so obvious why people talk. It lies beyond simple rational explanation. Under all the conflicting surface motives, it's almost as if the drive to confess is an instinct of its own. And here the movie benefits from its documentary reality. We are watching real exchanges, as close to what actually happened as screen time and reporters' notes will allow. This is how people really talk to the press. If it cannot be explained, perhaps it can be understood in the watching.

The film is a series of confessional set pieces, from types as varied as the highly principled Hugh Sloan and Jane Alexander's timid unnamed Bookkeeper to easy-living Donald Segretti, all revolving around Deep Throat, the most enigmatic source of all. The movie's plot strings the confrontations together in good detective-story fashion. It gives them story meaning, it derives ironies from the reporters' ruthlessness and energy from the reporters' implacable drive. But the exchanges themselves, not the plot, are the heart of the movie. If they are not compelling we don't keep watching. We saw that for ourselves when we ran the editor's first assembly, with its greased cuts. And that is the ultimate test for theme: what is the real reason we stay with the picture? What is the subliminal force that keeps us watching?

As it happens, this confessional urge is a perfect movie theme, precisely because it has to be seen to be understood. It is a fresh form of conflict, with built-in mystery and suspense. The reporters themselves don't know how it works. Even while they're pushing, they fear their source will dry up at any minute. They try everything to make people talk; sometimes nothing works, sometimes people unburden for what seems to be no reason at all. It is a mystery to them and to us. Every scene has the tension of the tentative exchange.

This kind of tension is ideal for drawing us in on an empathic level. We move back and forth between the characters within the tug-of-war of a scene. We feel the Bookkeeper's anguish, for instance, and listening to her we hope she will just shut up and not take any chances; then Bernstein speaks and we root for him to crack the case. So while on the surface this appears to be a film about Watergate, a dry and confusing subject, it is actually about characters caught in this unique relationship. It may be a plot-heavy voyeuristic film, but what holds us in our seats is our ambivalent, vicarious response to the characters. It was Pakula's great

contribution to the process that, consciously or unconsciously, he realized this was what his movie was about and he brought it to the screen. He made a voyeuristic film with a vicarious theme.

In this sense there is no such thing as a basically voyeuristic movie: the theme, the foundation on which the film is built, must be emotional. It may be vicarious or it may be visceral, but it must be an irreducible kernel of human nature, a particular case of a fundamental underlying problem we all struggle with in defining ourselves. In *All the President's Men* it is the human drive to speak the truth. In *2001* it is where we came from and where we are going and what that tells us about being human. In *Sophie's Choice* it is the struggle between hope and despair; in *Notorious* it is the conflict between love and duty; in *The Bridge on the River Kwai* it is the true demands of duty; in *The Magnificent Seven* it is what it means to be truly brave; in *Psycho* it is the murderous collision of lust and guilt. In a heavily visceral film it may be more cartoonish—the urge for revenge in *Dirty Harry*, *Rambo*, or countless others or heroic bravery in the face of impossible odds, like *Raiders of the Lost Ark*. The theme may be posed as a question, but it isn't a question that requires an answer, it is a dilemma we want to see acted out.

Movies can be made without themes. They're made all the time by producers who don't believe they need an emotional line to their film. They think a film can be about the greatest train robbery of all time or about saving the Super Bowl from terrorists. But I can't think of a movie that works that hasn't had a theme. Writers and directors assigned to such projects try to transplant a heart, and if they fail the movie dies on the table.

This no doubt sounds like a backward process, first to pick a movie idea and then to figure out what it's about. Yet it is standard operating procedure in Hollywood, and it has its own wacky logic. If you start with a gut-grabbing one-line idea, the thinking goes, there must be some way to translate its appeal into empathic terms (you can begin by asking why it grabs you); but if you start with a general empathic theme, say, the question "What is duty?" it is well nigh impossible to deduce a priori a story like *The Bridge on the River Kwai*.

Most novelists start from some concrete image or character or incident, some grain of sand that lodges in the mind and irritates the brain until it's covered with iridescent layers of story. It's hard to imagine a storyteller in any medium who doesn't. But novelists tend to take their work more seriously than movie industrialists take their film product. Novelists like to think their work has some larger meaning; most would be hard put to spend years writing a book that wasn't about something they thought was important. In Hollywood, producers and studio executives sometimes miss the connection between their great idea for a movie and the need for a theme to empower it. If the one-liner grabbed them, they might figure, it'll grab an audience. One of the main advantages of starting from a good novel when making a movie is that someone has already precipitated the theme out of the story. The backers don't have to be sold on its importance, and the screenwriter has it to fall back on.

Larger meaning aside, writers and directors cling to themes for a sound practical reason: themes tell them what to put in and what to leave out. With a theme, scenes and characters have a reason for being. If *The Magnificent Seven*, for example, were really about seven guys saving a town from bandits, who would the seven men be? What would happen to them? Sure, they would each specialize in a different weapon, there would be suspense and action, but what to show besides the shoot-outs? How to make one shoot-out different from the next?

Once the filmmakers decide that *The Magnificent Seven* is really about what it means to be brave, the process of constructing the film becomes less arbitrary and much clearer. We want a hero, the apotheosis of skill and bravery, at the center. Around him we want an array of types who evince different aspects of the human conflict between bravery and cowardice: a tough old pro who was once brave but fears he's lost his nerve (will he have what it takes when the chips are down?); a cocky greenhorn who thinks he's got what it takes but has never been tested; a braggart; a silent man of action; and, finally, the villagers themselves, scared rabbits willing to sell out their protectors to save their own hides (yet as Charles Bronson says they are the truly brave because they carry on their shoulders a huge rock called responsibility). The shoot-outs become ways for these men to test themselves; the plot becomes their successive steps toward their final inner confrontations. Notice that there is the same amount of action as in a themeless shoot-'em-up, maybe more. Since the human content makes each battle feel different, the audience will tire of gunplay less quickly.

Once we grant that a movie needs a theme, it is clear that the three worlds cannot operate in isolation. Under every voyeuristic scene of exposition, under every visceral action scene lurks the emotional content of the theme; but also, under every vicarious scene of character and feeling there lies the larger meaning, which, however emotional, must be inextricably bound up in the plot. For

OVERLEAF
The Magnificent Seven

the theme is only a theme if it empowers the action—if it drives the movie's story and gives it direction. In *The Bridge on the River Kwai*, for instance, when the plot has Jack Hawkins manipulate William Holden into returning behind Japanese lines to blow up the bridge, we are watching the story unfold but we are also watching Holden react to Hawkins' idea of duty. Back in the prison camp, when we see Sessue Hayakawa face off with Alec Guinness, trying to break his will, we have a scene of pure character confrontation —but at issue is the matter of their respective duties as British and Japanese officers, and at stake is the building of the bridge.

The better the script, the more the sense of interdependence. Just as a scene benefits from story compression, it gains from compressing the different ways of seeing as well. Most satisfying movie scenes engage us on at least two of our three levels at once. Hitchcock at his best cut and polished his scripts until they shone with the energy refracted between all three. In a movie like *Notorious* he and Ben Hecht get our minds working on all three levels in scene after scene, and as a result we lose ourselves completely in the film. We don't just watch it, we experience it.

Occasionally, a pure acting moment, a pure bit of visceral action, or a pure stretch of spectacle (as in *2001*) can be effective. But often films don't work because they lack Hitchcock's kind of complex compression. On the set, directors eager to make a scene work will focus on a single element; the dailies look fine, but when the film is put together the scene doesn't earn its way.

In shaping a film the choices are never clear. Is it better to shore up its weaknesses or spend that money and screen time exploiting its strengths? A perfectly constructed film can be a pale experience beside a film with a single strong element. *Klute*, for example, has

The Bridge on the River Kwai

an unexceptional mystery plot, a half-realized love affair and huge story holes, but Jane Fonda's Bree Daniels is so complex and compelling that the film is more satisfying than other more seamless detective stories. Here it was wise to spend the extra screen time on Bree rather than polish the story. The story might improve, but it will never justify the film; Bree Daniels will. In an imperfect world, that's saying a lot. The glass was half full, not half empty.

During editing it is always hard to tell how much is in the glass. One tends to overlook the parts that work, because they are problems that have been solved, and pore over the weakest parts. Then, in fixing what's wrong, directors and editors can sacrifice more important assets without realizing what they are giving up.

Even scenes that work might not belong in the picture. Does a certain character scene turn your detective movie into *Klute,* or does it just stop the story cold? Is an action scene the reason the audience will pay to see the movie, or is it a lengthy and exhausting digression from the real thrust of the story? Is a plot diabolically clever or so complicated the viewer doesn't have time to get to know the characters? The better the raw material, the tougher the decision.

Here a clear sense of theme makes all the difference. Just as a theme helps the writer decide what to put in, it helps the people editing the film decide what to take out—it tells them if a plot point matters, if a character scene is relevant, if an action scene pays its way. And if there is no clear idea of the theme yet, these fights about what belongs in the movie bring the confusion to light. Then with luck and hard work the theme will emerge, and the filmmakers will finally learn what their movie is all about.

OTHER FORMS

THE DOCUDRAMA

Docudrama" is a vague, ugly word for a bastard form, a hybrid some call sterile as a mule. Docudrama boasts that it is born of fact, as if all fiction weren't. It embodies a lie: we know it's make-believe, but we watch it because it pretends to be real. Yet like the mule, there are some jobs only the docudrama can do. Sometimes the line between fact and fiction demands to be blurred.

I must have been the first person calling himself a movie producer ever to set foot in Athens, Tennessee. I was there on a research junket with a writer, preparing a script for United Artists on the once notorious but long forgotten "Battle of Athens." Thirty-five years before, GIs returning home from World War II found their sleepy town in the grip of a corrupt Democratic machine. They tried to vote the pols out by forming a nonpartisan GI party, but armed hooligans stole the election. As the GIs were men of action, they broke into the local National Guard armory and with army weapons laid siege to the county jail, rousting the corrupt politicians in the act of stuffing ballot boxes behind the safety of its bars.

At the time it happened this so-called GI Insurrection sparked a national debate. Was it fascist or democratic? The incident was

OPPOSITE PAGE
TOP: Patrick Dempsey (*left*) from *In the Mood* and the real Ellsworth "Sonny" Wisecarver that he portrayed. BOTTOM: *The Last Emperor*

front-page news all over America. It is easy to forget, but people then were just as worried about the return of war-crazed veterans as they were after Vietnam. And after World War II the returning troops didn't number in the hundreds of thousands, they numbered in the millions. Was the Athens rebellion a sign that these legions of hardened fighters threatened the fabric of democracy? Or were they free men standing up for their rights?

The writer, Howard Chesley, and I had read the newspaper accounts, and we knew that the leader of the GIs was a handsome fellow named Big Jim Buttram, a storekeeper's son, who had served in Patton's honor guard during the war. After their initial uncertainty, the press had decided that the GIs' action was in defense of liberty, and Big Jim was anointed a national hero; President Eisenhower rewarded him with the postmastership of Athens.

We met Jim when he was six months from retirement, seated flanked by flags behind his desk at the post office. Most people's blood would stir if a couple of guys from Hollywood came along and said they wanted to make a major studio movie about their life. Vanity would out, perhaps followed quickly by greed. But much to my surprise Jim was politely distant. He didn't look with enthusiasm on the idea of our making him a hero all over again. He didn't have anything to say about the old days, and he absolutely was not interested in signing a release.

The release, of course, was my big concern as producer on the project. We could make the movie without it, but what we could show would be severely restricted. The law says we have the right to dramatize public events, but it doesn't look kindly on our selling tickets to people's private lives without their permission.

When we paid a courtesy call on the newly elected sheriff, he echoed Big Jim's response. He was the first Democrat to hold the office since the Battle of Athens, and he warned us that folks around there didn't want the old wounds reopened. He was right. We spent a couple of weeks talking to people and meeting the same guarded response. I collected what releases I could, but I knew that Big Jim's cooperation was the key to the story.

Finally, the day before we were to leave, we broke through the silence. A fellow named Bill White showed up in our motel room with a six-pack of beer and announced that the story we'd been told was a lie. *He* was the real hero of the Battle of Athens. He'd checked with a lawyer, he said, and had been told that after thirty-five years the statute of limitations had run out on the various crimes that were committed that night, and he wanted to set the record straight.

White was no middle-class honor guard, he was a hillbilly, part Indian, leatherneck marine who had fought his way across the Pacific. He showed us magazine photos of himself killing a wild boar with a spear. Jim Buttram, it turned out, was the figurehead erected by a clever Republican politician who had died soon thereafter, Ralph Duggan. Duggan, also a returning vet but a more patrician sort, saw the GIs as a way to break the grip of his Democratic rivals and restore the Republicans to power. He figured the GI party would last one election, just long enough to oust the incumbents and pave the way for the Republicans' return (which is just what happened). Duggan didn't figure on Bill White's taking the whole thing so much to heart that he'd ransack the armory with some of his rowdier friends and start shelling the county jail. This led the (Democratic) governor to call out the National Guard. Only the Guard's refusal to shoot on fellow GIs prevented a pitched battle.

When the smoke cleared, Bill had indeed saved the day, but it wasn't at all plain whether the GIs would be hailed as heroes or sent to prison. Duggan persuaded Bill to lay low and let Buttram, who was appalled by the violence and had nothing to do with it, take the "credit." (If the law took out after the GIs, Bill was an obvious victim, whereas Buttram could prove he hadn't been involved.) Bill, a man used to living on the fringe, didn't take much convincing. The small town hung together, and the hordes of journalists who descended to cover the story (including Theodore White) were all sold the saga of brave Jim Buttram and the GI Non-Partisan League.

Bill's story rang true; to our delight, it checked out. Now there was some real meat to the movie. But as the story looked better and better, my release receded farther away. Bill White was glad to sign, but how would we ever get Big Jim now? I thought he'd have to be crazy to let us expose the scam.

I had reckoned without Howard Chesley, who had developed his powers of persuasion when he worked his way through college selling stereos. He had a hunch. On our way out of town he wanted to stop by the post office for one last crack at Big Jim.

Big Jim greeted us with relief when we told him we were leaving. Had we got what we needed, he asked? Yes, I said. And then Howard spoke up. He wanted Big Jim to know that we had talked to Bill

White, and we were going to tell what really happened. Would Jim sign our release?

Jim sagged visibly when he realized we knew the truth. And he agreed to sign. What Howard had seen was that Jim wasn't afraid of the truth, he was sick of living the lie, of being the butt of local ironies about brave Big Jim. Even thirty-five years later, Jim welcomed the chance to end the charade.

One last stop—Jim's wife. She was a big, gentle woman. We told her we had his release, and we asked if she would sign too. She signed, I think more in deference to her husband than because she thought it was a good idea, and then she fixed me with her soft eyes and said, "You won't do anything to hurt my Jim, will you?"

Of all the projects that got away, this is the one that I've always felt should damn well have been made. Yet when I think about Jim's wife, I'm relieved it never quite got off the ground. Maybe I shouldn't be telling the story now. But Jim Buttram wanted us to tell the truth. Here I can come as close as I know how. By the time we were finished making a movie, who knows what violence would have been done to the man's integrity?

One of the axioms of deal making is that it is easier to sell a true story than something made up. Studio executives, like everyone else, have their doubts, and it's more persuasive to hawk them a movie about a priest who pushes cocaine if you've got a newspaper clipping that tells the sorry tale. This doesn't mean the studio executives expect you to *tell* the real story. Far from it. Once the decision is made, they expect you to crank it to the limit for maximum drama. But somehow knowing there is a kernel of truth is very reassuring.

The studio exec has a good point when it comes to playing fast and loose with the truth. It is easy to become enamored of a story just because it is true, and it is very dangerous if you do. From the writer's point of view, the great advantage of the true story is that life has done the writer's work. Actuality can supply characters, events, and even dialogue. But often the lure of the true story is that it is so bizarre, so unheard-of, that no one has ever seen it done before. While this is an asset to the tale it is also a sign that the story will be hard to realize. Simply because an event is true doesn't mean it is believable, and if the filmmakers have picked one because it's incredible they are going to have trouble selling it to their viewers no matter how many times they tell them it's true. After all, the audience doesn't have any particular reason to believe them.

When Phil Alden Robinson wrote the gentle romantic comedy *In the Mood*, he based it on the true tale of Sonny Wisecarver, a fifteen-year-old who eloped twice with older women. Proud of how closely he had hewed to the truth, Robinson prefaced his film with the voice of the adult Sonny saying "This film is true." But when Robinson tested the film with audiences, he found they didn't believe him. So he rewrote the opening for Sonny to say, "This film is true, as best as I can remember it," and the audience, comfortable it wasn't being sold the whole truth, found the film more credible.

Sometimes the very events the writer fastens onto because they make a subject theatrical are the ones that don't work in the finished story. An incident that sticks out as crude in Robinson's film is a courtroom scene in which a judge orders the boy's penis measured to see if he is "normal." The scene seems to be dropped in for an easy laugh, and it threatens the tone of the piece. Robinson swears the scene is real. Would he have put the scene in if he had made up the story?

Robinson's next film, *Field of Dreams*, was based on W. P. Kinsella's novel *Shoeless Joe*. Critics have singled out some speeches in it as being old-fashioned, too much in the spirit of forties movies. This time they came straight from the book. But there is a crucial difference between the scene from life and the scene from a book. Robinson left the *Shoeless Joe* speeches in, in spite of studio concerns, because he felt they summed up what the film was all about. He was borrowing not just the story from the book but its theme, and that is something a novel can give which can never be gotten from life. In adapting a true story, it is up to the screenwriter to give reality a theme. And then reality is profoundly altered.

Crass as it seems, in most "true" stories there is little or nothing at stake if the writer changes them to suit the needs of the drama. The only people who care are the actual participants, if they are still alive. And once they have granted the filmmakers permission to invade their privacy, they are as likely as not to prefer myth to reality. It will certainly be more exciting, and it will probably make them feel more important because to recast a real event as a drama the writer has to simplify, reduce the number of characters, and make the central protagonist as active as possible. Making *All the*

OVERLEAF
The Killing Fields

President's Men, for instance, we had to eliminate an editor from the story, even though the book acknowledged his role as crucial. To my knowledge he was the only person at the *Post* who voiced real dislike for the finished movie. Does it matter how true *The Untouchables* is, or *Hoosiers* or *Conrack* or *In the Mood*, or *Stand and Deliver*, or *Serpico*, or *Tucker*, or *The French Connection* or *Butch Cassidy and the Sundance Kid?*

All the President's Men, however, was more than an idea sold by clippings. Like *The Last Emperor* or *Patton* or *Silkwood* or *The Longest Day* or *The Right Stuff*, it is a true docudrama: the historical importance of the event is a principal reason to make the movie. Here the responsibility to reality is greater because the movie deserves to be judged partly by how well it illuminates history. When the facts are twisted too far to fit film drama, as when *Mississippi Burning* ignores the contribution of black civil rights workers, the satisfaction of watching the film erodes, no matter how well the film works in its own terms.

But even these docudramas must still be dramas first. They are liable to suffer from a second misconception of the form, namely, the idea that an event is worth watching simply because it's important. These stories too must be ruthlessly shaped into fiction, even if there are lawyers on the set checking the dialogue for accuracy, as there were on *All the President's Men*.

Because they imply more truth than they deliver, docudramas are dangerous weapons; when they are made by people whose only use for truth is to hook their audience, they are dangerous weapons in the hands of children. But the same power that can make them grossly misleading also gives them the unique ability to provide historical insight. Film triggers so many responses on so many different levels that seeing *The Battle of Algiers* or *The Killing Fields* is an experience of another order than reading even the most impassioned account.

Unlike documentaries, docudramas take the liberties of fiction to put the viewer at the decisive moment of the decisive event. The filmmakers can pick exactly where they want to be when, and they can intensify the event by compressing it. Any moviemaking has to be selective. In a documentary, even if the cameraman is at the right place at the right time, condensing a two-hour meeting into a two-minute scene means showing a series of confusing and disconnected fragments; the docudrama, however, can sculpt the bits into a continuous scene that feels natural in the context of drama. At its best the docudrama can be a translation from one language to another, from the disjointed, amorphous language of living experience to the more compact, structured conventions of an experience observed.

But the docudrama's real value is that it asks a question historians shun: the emotional why. Not what a person did, not even his or her motives from the point of view of practical self-interest or raison d'état, but what the person was feeling when he acted. If our day-to-day life is ruled by emotional subtext, why shouldn't grand moments of history be? A trained historian cannot in good conscience speculate on something this amorphous without solid evidence, but it is a question of inescapable value—perhaps the most important question.

Like it or not, the docudrama writer has to face down this question in order to construct his scene. To write characters without private motives is to deny that people act for personal reasons, and that is the most misleading portrayal of all. One might argue that the writer's opinion in this matter is of no value, that his solution is an insult to history and watching it a waste of time; I would reply that the alternative is not asking the question, and that is worse. If the writer is steeped in the subject and trying to be honest, the writer's answer is bound to be thought-provoking at the very least. Even if it is wrong, a new question has been asked. And as scientists say, fresh insight comes not from new answers but from new questions.

When I was writing a docudrama on Iran, for instance, I came across an incident in the life of the Ayatollah Khomeini I knew I had to dramatize. The Shah, at the height of his power, once sent police to Khomeini's house to arrest him. The Ayatollah could have fled in a car out a back alley, but he refused. Instead, he hid in a neighboring building, where he sat for an hour listening to his servants scream while the police tried to beat them into confessing his whereabouts. Finally, Khomeini went into the street and gave himself up.

A scene packed with drama but demanding explanation. I had to give Khomeini a reason for his behavior. If he was going to give himself up, why did he wait so long? Was he simply afraid, first thinking he could hide out and then changing his mind when he heard the screams? But then why didn't he escape immediately? He had the chance. And if he was going to give himself up anyway, why let his servants be brutally beaten for over an hour?

A historian might avoid the question, but I had to find an answer before I could write the scene. According to his official biographer,

The Birth of a Nation

Khomeini had locked himself in his hiding place and then lost the key. Apparently, it took him an hour of searching in the small, sparsely furnished room before he finally found the key he himself had hidden under a carpet. This I found hard to believe. It smacked of the historian's contrivance—by blaming the incident on chance it deftly sidestepped the human question and kept the motive of the sainted Khomeini shrouded from view.

I chose another explanation, based on what I had learned of the man. Khomeini stayed in that room on purpose. Not that he was afraid. He did not scare easily, and arrest would only have enhanced his reputation. But he wasn't about to give himself up immediately either. He wanted to create an incident. He wanted to make his servants into martyrs for his cause.

I had no hard evidence this was true, but when it came to me I knew I was going to build my scene around it. True or false, it summed up the man for me. The scene was now more than an isolated event, it became a way of explaining Khomeini to the audience—a ruthless man, uncompromising, driven by a higher purpose for which he would sacrifice others as willingly as he would sacrifice himself. The scene became a metaphor for his life struggle.

The better the work, the less the "docudrama" label matters one way or the other. The best docudrama blurs into the best historical fiction. If Shakespeare had been in the Writers' Guild, CBS would have marketed his histories as a docudrama miniseries on the English kings. Is there a work of history which tells us more about Napoleon's invasion of Russia than *War and Peace?* Does anybody think of *Lawrence of Arabia* as a docudrama? *The Birth of a Nation?* Woodrow Wilson said the D. W. Griffith film was "like history written with lightning. And it's all true."

THE DOCUMENTARY

In Hollywood, documentaries are viewed as a form of punishment. If you commit a crime, if you forge a check or are caught with cocaine, the judge will sentence you to make a documentary. But when, as a disaffected architecture student, I first took the plunge into movies, documentaries were my passion. Not that I particularly enjoyed watching them. I wanted to make them.

I had been one of those teenagers who hid from adolescence behind a still camera; my Leica let me feel like a superior observer instead of an incompetent participant in my own rites of passage. When I finally started making documentary films I was working from the same adolescent impulses. I thought the only way I could get power and control was by being the outsider, the trenchant observer whose point of view matters because he's telling it like it is. I chased the fantasy of the Lone Filmmaker, beholden to no one, producing, directing, shooting, editing, doing it all himself—but while I labored like an artist obsessed, the appeal of the documentary was that the other guy, the subject, was really doing the work. He made the movie special. He was the reality, I was the mirror.

My power lay in being invisible. The audience had to feel it was watching the reality, not a fun-house reflection; for fun-house reflections they would go to a regular movie. Being invisible was, of course, a highly manipulative operation. I had to have an attitude toward the material, some point I was trying for, but I had to make the viewers think they were making the discoveries themselves, not having the discoveries foisted upon them.

Richard Leacock, D. A. Pennebaker, and the Maysles Brothers were the American apostles of this pure, "*vérité* style," "direct cinema," which became possible after the invention in the midsixties of the Eclair NPR and the converted Auricon cameras, the first light, quiet sixteen-millimeter cameras to allow for professional sync-sound recording. For the first time, the cameraman and the sound recordist, just the two of them, could take their equipment and film anyone anywhere. Subjects might find it disquieting to be followed about by two heavily armed technicians, but eventually people adapt to just about anything. If the filmmakers were willing to spend the time and the film, to hang around long enough, their subjects did seem to forget they were there. Then the filmmakers could go back home, sort through the miles of intimate, spontaneous footage, and piece together a picture of the way things really were. So the theory went.

In the hands of masters, these techniques resulted in a series of remarkable films, like Leacock-Pennebaker's Bob Dylan documentary *Don't Look Back* and the Maysles Brothers' *Salesman*, a look at Bible sellers. While these films bore little outward resemblance to the Hollywood extravaganza—at the time they were viewed as iconoclastic challenges to the movie establishment—on a craft level the goal was the same: be invisible. Don't let the filmmaking get in the way of the film. Shape your viewers' reactions without letting them feel manipulated. And though the techniques were tightly circumscribed, the fundamental problems were the same as the Hollywood film's: how to compress time, reveal character, tell a story, move the audience. As it turned out, *vérité* filmmaking was an excellent introduction to Hollywood filmmaking.

The documentary filmmaker's edge is the presumption that what the audience is seeing is real. Unless viewers are given reason to think otherwise, they will give him the benefit of the doubt. A viewer can't say, "That couldn't happen" or "He wouldn't do that" because the filmmaker can reply, "Ah, but it did, and he does."

Maintaining the illusion of reality can be very confining. Hollywood filmmakers must keep their space clearly defined, as if the viewer, through the camera, were almost another character present in the scene. In *vérité* filmmaking the camera really is another person, a man or woman lugging a twenty-pound gizmo and a battery pack who stands right next to the subjects in the scene. The camera watches what transpires, and we watch with it. The cameraman can walk around, use the zoom lens, turn the camera on or off. Anything we see that can't happen that way is faked, and to knowledgeable viewers it is proof that they're not watching reality at all but some construct cobbled together to feel dramatic.

Albert and David Maysles filming *Grey Gardens*.

In a true *vérité* scene, the film is at the mercy of the moment-to-moment sensibility of the cameraman. Take the bane of *vérité* filmmaking, the bobble. If you have ever seen hand-held documentaries, you have had cause to shut your eyes and shake out the dizziness that comes from watching scenes sway as the cameraman moves about. It takes practice for a cameraman to realize the extent of the problem because while shooting, bobbles aren't disorienting. Through the viewfinder, the place stays put and the frame floats around. But to viewers, watching the film projected within a fixed frame, the space bobs and weaves. Their eyes work to keep the horizon steady, as if they were on a sail-boat, and the result is a form of cinematic seasickness. The great hand-held cameramen have the sure, steady hands of a surgeon; for the others, wide-angle lenses diminish the queasy effect and tripods eliminate it entirely. Editing a scene with camera bobbles is a painful but effective introduction to the demands of movie space.

Shooting *vérité*, the cameraman must instantaneously make the same crucial decision that a director or an editor mulls over at leisure in planning or editing a dramatic film: "Who do we want to be on?" In a documentary, when someone talks, the camera focuses on him; if someone else across the room draws a gun, we won't know about it until shouts bring it to the cameraman's attention—or the head of the person being interviewed explodes.

Documentary camerawork is good training for theatrical directing because it teaches cameramen to be decisive and trust their instincts. For me the greatest satisfactions of documentary work were those moments I felt an almost mystical connection with my subjects—when I felt so much a part of the event I was shooting that I seemed to know what was going to happen before they knew, when I moved as part of the flow, not as an observer reacting after the fact.

The sensation is astonishing: a calm, clear-eyed alignment with the currents of the universe. It is no wonder *vérité* was the documentary style of the sixties. My first paying job in the movie business was projecting dailies for *Woodstock*, and when things were rough, cameraman-director Michael Wadleigh would cheer himself up by running a nearly perfect roll of documentary film, a single ten-minute take he shot onstage with the group Canned Heat. It was perfectly choreographed, almost as if the group had rehearsed for the camera—Wadleigh, perhaps the best hand-held cameraman of them all, had moved from musician to musician unerringly, without a bobble, always anticipating; at the end, when a fan climbed onstage, we saw the lead singer hug the fan, give the guy a cigarette, and hold off the security guards—without him or Wadleigh missing a beat. Shooting it must have been a hell of a high, as we said in those days.

The scene never made it to the finished film. Canned Heat wasn't a big enough group to warrant ten minutes of screen time, and the song couldn't be shortened. It was shot too well. This is a common problem in *vérité* filming; in fact, it is a commonplace among makers of *vérité* documentaries that the very best footage will end up on the floor.

Cheating is tempting. Often a scene will work better if it is shortened, but the compression must be concealed from the audience. If extraneous film is simply cut out, the people on the screen will suddenly pop from one position to another, creating a distracting "jump cut." The scene will feel jerky and abridged. Jump cuts can be smoothed over by showing something else in between, say a close-up of a person listening who isn't changing position, so when we cut back to the original angle we think people have moved while we weren't watching and we believe we're still experiencing the scene in unabridged real time. This feels more continuous, but to those who care about these things it is instantly recognizable as a cheat. The filmmaker is implying that the scene happened faster than it really did, and who knows what he is leaving out?

That second shot, called a "cutaway" because it allows the editor to cut away and then return to the first shot, had to come from somewhere. When was it shot? In our example, it's a shot of someone listening. But what is he listening to? Not what we show him listening to. The camera wasn't on him then, it was on the jump-cut scene. So if he is reacting to what he hears—if he's angry, say—we're creating a reaction which didn't exist. We are implying he was angry when he might have been delighted.

This problem is compounded by the temptations of storytelling. If an expedition crossing a rickety rope bridge in the Andes is being filmed, for example, it is much more dramatic—and better storytelling—to show the leader work his way across the dangerous chasm from an angle where we can see his face and really watch what he's doing. That is, shoot him from the front. But how to get in front of him? By crossing the bridge first. Now the leader isn't the first person across, the cameraman is, and any narration or dialogue of the "Will it hold?" variety—or even the unstated implication—is simply hogwash. Almost every adventure documentary has shots of this "Where did they put the camera?" sort. Sometimes they even show mountain climbers conquering peaks for the first time—shot from the top of the mountain.

You might well ask what difference it makes. It's only a movie. You have to put your faith in the taste and judgment of the filmmaker, no matter what kind of movie you are watching. The answer is that the *vérité* film promises more. It claims to show not some director's idea of reality but what really happened. We trust *vérité* filmmakers because they're straight with us; the minute they shade the game their judgment comes into question. Then we only side with them because we agree with their prejudices.

Even the best *vérité* filmmaking is inherently contradictory. Life doesn't imitate art that closely. In trying to fulfill our expectations of movie drama while at the same time showing things as they really are, filmmakers are forced to shape life to fit movie scenes with movie pace, movie structure, and movie conflict. For all its pretensions to objectivity, to showing us the unvarnished truth, the labor involved in cramming life into dramatic form can be more distorting than presenting it in bits connected by jump cuts or narration. At least the point of view of the disjointed version is less insidious.

Frederick Wiseman is the reigning American master of "direct" cinema. In films like *Titicut Follies* (about a mental institution), *High School, Law and Order, Basic Training*, and *Near Death*, he explores our social institutions with a sharp eye and a deft sense of human drama. His films are infused with his very specific sensibility, a feeling for how society tries to mold the individual to its own ends and how people stand up to the coercion. Let's just say Wiseman doesn't take kindly to pressures for conformity.

His shooting ratio, which is within the normal range for *vérité* work, is about thirty to one, that is, for every hour of screen time he shoots thirty hours of film. Much as I admire his work, I can't help asking myself when I watch his films if someone else could have drawn a very different picture from the other twenty-nine hours of film. And how did he decide what to shoot in the first place? In *High School*, say, did he randomly pick the teachers he concentrated on? Am I learning as much about Wiseman's attitude toward authority as I am about the institution?

Wiseman movies work because they transcend the form. I trust his instincts the way I trust Truffaut's instincts or Hitchcock's, but his success doesn't mean his films are any more "real" than *Noto-*

High School

rious. His techniques are merely more deceptive. In Wiseman's words, "I readily acknowledge that my films are biased, subjective, condensed, compressed . . . but I think that my films are fair. And by fair I mean that they are an accurate account of the experience I had when making the film rather than an imposition of a preconceived point of view."

But we all have "preconceived points of view"; that's what makes us who we are. One of the dangers of this form of filmmaking is that in selecting what seems most "real," most representative, from miles of footage, it is possible to fool yourself into thinking you have been objective, when in fact you have made the film without ever confronting your own prejudices. I learned this the hard way on a film I fervently believed in, a documentary on an experiment in teaching architecture and town planning to fifth-graders.

The idea of the program was that in the process of exploring, mapping, and redesigning their own neighborhood, and finally building a model of their results, the kids could learn their basic curriculum and the design process to boot. It was led by two guest instructors, the project director, an experienced teacher who had pioneered the technique in her own classroom, and her brother, a gifted architect, and they were supposed to work in collaboration with the students' regular teacher.

The project made me wish I was in the fifth grade again. The kids were challenged but also encouraged. Because they were using their skills for a recognizable goal, redesigning their neighborhood, all the math, mapmaking, and studying of how cities worked made real sense. The kids were charming and enthusiastic, and I shot my film with pleasure, thinking I was making a good film while helping promote a good cause.

And then one day all hell broke loose. It was a day intended to be stressful, the beginning of the real design process. Each child had mapped out his or her own plot of land, and now when they put them together they discovered that there were no streets that connected and no houses, factories, or stores to speak of. All the girls had drawn schools and all the boys football fields. This precipitated a classic design conflict: everyone agreed that there was too much of a good thing, but none of the kids was willing to give up her school or his stadium. The experience was supposed to convince them to get together and work out a master plan.

All this happened more or less as anticipated, and it looked fine to me while I filmed it. On the way out the door, though, while I was filming the project head and the architect, I noticed that the classroom teacher was looking disgruntled and I asked her what was wrong. She demurred, but I pressed her and finally it all came out: the teacher was worried about what she saw as the anarchic direction the planning was taking; she thought the kids were being manipulated. She accused the project head of rigging the class election for town mayor (apparently the project head had selected the student she thought would be best and coached the girl on what to say, unbeknownst to me). She accused the project head of tossing away a child's work, which prompted a passionate denial. Before the conversation was over, the teacher had thrown the architect and the project head out of her classroom and told them never to return. I filmed away in a state of shock, trying to keep in focus and not jiggle too much, prodding with the occasional question while I tried to figure out what had gone wrong and what would become of my film.

When the dust settled, I understood. I had caused this. To be sure, the teacher had her own reasons for feeling anxious. She was used to problems with answers, and her sense of teacherly rightness was threatened by the design process (which she herself had never been taught) in which there are no right answers, only workable compromises to fundamentally insoluble problems. But the real underlying difficulty was as much my fault as anyone's. The teacher felt left out.

The camera had changed the equation. Once I got my grant to document their work, this had stopped being a teaching experiment and become a chance for the project designers to embalm their technique on film. This was their chance to record for posterity (and to proselytize), and the project leader and the architect wanted to be sure everything went exactly as it should. They didn't have anything against the teacher, they just wanted her out of the way so they could show the full potential of their project. So, with the best will in the world, the project became a process of media manipulation in which I was a willing if unwitting partner. It would have continued that way, no doubt, had we not forgotten rule one of the public school system: the teacher is monarch of her classroom. Interlopers proceed at the peril of her displeasure. We ignored her and paid the price.

In some ways my film was better off than before. I had been making a valentine to the project; now that I had real conflict on film I had the key to something a lot less insipid. But I needed two more things. I needed to set up the conflict and pay it off.

I realized just how much I had been a party to the process when I went back over my dailies, looking for the setup. In all my thousands of feet of film I had only two shots of the teacher working with the kids and one shot of her looking disgruntled. Like the program designers, I had blocked her out. I hadn't planned to ignore her; she just hadn't been doing much that I thought merited my attention.

Well, I could fill in with interviews, I thought, if I could only get an ending. Luckily, thanks to the camera, the teacher vowed to continue on her own. She had done art projects before, she said, and she knew a designer she would bring in. So I figured I'd film the teacher talking about her problems with the project, film her finishing it her way, then show the film to the architect and project head and film their comments. Maybe I could come up with something about what went wrong that would show by contrast how it should have worked.

The teacher had in a sense achieved her aim. Now that my film was about the clash, she had gone from being a bit player to a leading role. To balance my conflict I needed her to be as open and articulate as her opposite numbers.

Unfortunately, she wasn't. And again I was reaping what I had sown. She didn't realize how much I now needed two strong opposing views. She couldn't believe my sudden conversion from ignoring her to hanging on her every word. She thought I was setting her up. So though she allowed me to film her, she spoke in bland generalities, the way she had seen educators talk on TV.

I did the best I could. The teacher brought in a designer who liked kids but saw the experiment as a lark. As the architect said when I showed him the footage, "He didn't take the kids seriously so they didn't take themselves seriously." By the end, this ambitious city-building project became a pretty Styrofoam park sprinkled with cute buildings.

The architect and project head were as articulate as the teacher was stolid. They deftly skewered all her mistakes; the only disquieting note was the obvious pleasure they took in her failure. (This is where *vérité* film adds an extra dimension. To hear them talk, they were disconsolate and dismayed; to watch them talk they were delighted.)

What saved the film was the children. When the project was over I had them show me around their "city," and they talked with pride at first about their peace building in the shape of a dove and their rooftop restaurant, but soon their disappointment surfaced. "This isn't a city," one girl said, "it's just a bunch of pretty buildings." They had learned enough before the blowup to know what they had missed out on.

I ended the movie with the kids' own testimony, trying to capture their sense of being cheated, to portray them as the innocent victims of adult battles. In the end, the film came to be about how when educators fight, their students pay the price.

In all, a humbling experience. Not only had my filmmaking poisoned the experiment I was supposed to document, but even if it hadn't, if the fight had never surfaced and I had finished as planned, I would have made a film I believed in which didn't tell the true story at all. How many other documentaries are made that way?

Was the film successful? Certainly my funders would have preferred a happy film. I ran it once for the top administrators of the National Endowment for the Arts, who had commissioned both the experiment and the movie; Nancy Hanks, their chief, called the film "thought-provoking." To my knowledge that was the first and last time they ever used it. When I asked permission to submit it to a film festival on architectural education I received a stern letter forbidding me.

But at the next funding cycle the NEA allocated an additional $300,000 for teacher preparation.

The problem of ambiguous reality, of the need to trust a tale-bearer who shouldn't even trust himself, is a problem common to any form of journalism. But it is more insidious in documentary films, particularly *vérité* films, because the filmmakers stash themselves out of sight behind images of the event. The viewer thinks that because he is seeing real incidents, he is learning what really happened. The strength, the immediacy of the documentary image, is a potential trap for viewer and filmmaker alike.

And sometimes images aren't enough. Good as documentaries are at showing things, as a nonfiction medium they suffer from a fundamental weakness: they're just not much good at telling things. Film does a poor job of communicating information.

First, it's slow: we read words much faster than we hear them, and on film it seems they must be spoken at their slowest if we want to catch their whole meaning. Fact-filled documentaries are not Wiseman-style slices of life: the usual way to give facts in documentaries is either narration or the "talking head." The rule of thumb for writing dense narration is four words per foot of 16mm film, or about one hundred and forty words a minute. That means a twenty-five-minute film of nonstop fast narration would hold about 3,500 words, or ten pages of this book.

Second, no film can come close to wall-to-wall narration and make any sense. Unlike books and magazines, movies are time-locked. The viewer can't choose the pace and can't thumb back through to pick up what was missed, even though it is not humanly possible to pay strict attention for the whole length of a film. The filmmakers must give the viewer a chance to pick up lost threads, which means they have to warn the viewer when important ideas are coming and repeat them afterward to make sure they've registered. In practice, that ten pages of information in a twenty-five-minute film becomes more like five.

Third and most important, words can never prevail in a film. Words are by nature of the medium handmaiden to the images. If we see a dog bark and hear a meow, we may laugh—but we have no doubt we are watching a dog. Picture overpowers sound, and the eye outpaces the ear. We process visual information so much faster than we process sound that while the ear is listening to the slow drumbeat of words, the eye is impatiently scanning for fresh images.

A lecture on film doesn't work any better than a play on film. I am a fan of the books of the late mythologist Joseph Campbell, for example, and I looked forward to his one-hour television interviews with Bill Moyers. But watching them taxed my self-discipline to the limit. Try as I might I kept nodding off.

And then I got hooked. Why? What grabbed my interest wasn't what he was saying, I discovered, but the man who was saying it. He radiated a kind of cheerful fatalism. Here was a man who understood what life was all about. If I looked deep enough into those twinkling eyes, maybe I would too.

What keeps us watching a talking-head documentary is the same thing that holds us when we watch talking heads, otherwise known as close-ups, in a theatrical film: subtext. Not what the person is saying but what he is feeling. Bad as film is for expressing facts or ideas, it is unparalleled for conveying emotion.

If we see faces on the screen, we cannot help but search them for their true feelings; if they're the faces of Indian street urchins, as in *Faces of Calcutta*, the film is riveting. That documentary is no more than a series of close-ups of children talking in monotone to the camera. But while they matter-of-factly describe their desperate lives, we search their smooth features for signs of their daily struggle, we admire the prosaic bravery in their manner, we project ourselves and our children into their stony stares. Our eyes have plenty to do while our ears our listening.

Most of Errol Morris' two-hour film *The Thin Blue Line* consists of a mere handful of shots, and talking heads at that, but it rarely feels static or slow. At first we meet a sardonic man in a prison uniform, Randall Adams, with the looks and the flat, impassive wit of a serious Bob Newhart. He is very calm, but we sense it is a calm born of desperation as he tells his story. It appears from what he says that he is falsely accused of murder. He certainly wants us to think so, and the more we learn of the case, the more we are inclined to believe him.

While we are still getting oriented, maybe fifteen minutes into the movie, when we are tilting in Adams' direction but still not convinced of his innocence, he tells how he was hauled in by the police for questioning and handed a confession to sign. When he refused, Adams says, the detective left and returned with a gun, presumably the murder weapon. "Look at the gun," he was told. He looked. "Pick it up." He wouldn't. At this point, Adams says, the detective pulled a police revolver, cocked it, and pointed it at him. "Pick it up." They stared at each other for a long time. "I don't enjoy having guns pointed at me," Adams dryly observes. But Adams didn't want his fingerprints on the murder weapon either. "Finally, when he realized he would have to kill me before I would pick up the gun, he put away his revolver." At this moment Morris abruptly cuts from Adams telling his story to the detective in question, looking us straight in the eye, every inch a cop, saying defensively, "We had a friendly conversation."

Waves of bitter laughter rippled through the theater where I saw the film. We, the audience, had the pleasure of sitting in judgment on these two men, and we were not fooled one bit by this cop's idea of "a friendly conversation." Though our only evidence was the men's conflicting testimony, we knew exactly what was going on. We were reading these men the way we read actors, testing for motive and emotional truth. Only here the process was overt and we were not judging performance, we were judging their true character.

Compared to an in-depth piece of investigative journalism, *The Thin Blue Line* hits only the highlights of the tale, but for a film it is packed with information. On one level we are having a voyeuristic experience digging out the real story, but that is not what compels us to watch those faces for two hours. The real fascination isn't the mystery puzzle the facts present but the light they throw on the personalities in the film: who is the opportunist, who the idealist, who the innocent victim, who got away with murder. We can watch those faces because we are having a vicarious experience, an empathic exchange with the characters. This may seem obvious, but all too many documentaries miss the point.

During the revolver story Morris gooses his audience with a trick purists would despise. As Adams is finishing his version of events— seconds before the film cuts to the detective—the filmmaker inserts a big close-up of a police revolver being cocked and pointed at the audience. While this shot is hardly evidence, it has the effect of evidence. It persuades us that Adams is telling the truth, so when the detective contradicts him in the next shot we are sure the cop is lying. Adams' story is tense, real, involving. When it ends with a

gun pointed at us we get a visceral twinge of fear—that's how it feels for a cop to push a loaded weapon in *our* face. Our laughter at the cop's line is as much visceral release as vicarious irony.

Michael Moore took liberties one step further in *Roger and Me*, his scathingly satiric look at the human costs of General Motors' pullout from Flint, Michigan. He offended purist critics by making a slanted, polemical film; yet the film was popular with audiences and to my mind an honest, effective piece of filmmaking because he made it without the inherent hypocrisy of *vérité* technique. He didn't only admit his bias, he wallowed in it. He played his own curmudgeonly outrage for laughs and the result is a tough and amusing film—which people want to see—that makes a strong case for his point of view by capitalizing on the very one-sidedness in question. He made himself a character the audience enjoyed living through vicariously.

For me, documentaries have always played well on television. They seem to suffer least from the small screen, partly because they often depend more heavily on words than on images but more, I think, because so few have a visceral component. If TV is movies without the visceral, then documentaries are perfect for the medium. Even Morris must stage (some would say fake) the visceral scene to get his effect.

But while TV is short on the visceral, it has a compensating power. On film there may be confusion between what is real and what is staged, but there is never any suggestion that what we're watching is happening then and there as we watch it. Not so with video. If we turn on the TV and see Robert Kennedy shot or the *Challenger* blowing up, there is no way to tell from the image whether we're watching it live, in instant replay, or on the tenth anniversary of the tragedy. This gives the videotape image an immediacy film can never have—it creates the illusion in us that what we are watching is not only real but happening before our very eyes. Live. A tape show like *Cops*, the Fox network's weekly documentary on the Miami police filmed with portable video cameras, takes on an unnerving transparency.

Film or tape, since we see the documentary through the cameraman's eye and what is being filmed is real, we can only get the point-of-view sort of visceral, gut-wrenching experience if the person shooting the film is going through hell himself. Cameramen are known as daredevils, but even cameramen don't consider films worth dying for. When the cameraman does find himself in a life-or-death situation, covering a war or a wildfire, the effect is unpredictable. Sometimes real danger pales beside the Hollywood counterpart: the enemy is a distant fuzzy blur, the threat is diffuse, real guns sound like popguns. Sometimes the reality is shattering. Always it is overlaid with the awareness of the person behind the camera, risking life and limb for real to bring us our kicks. As in theatrical footage of stunts that ended tragically, the film is too bound up with real suffering for us to give ourselves wholeheartedly to its visceral emotions.

Some documentaries, like the mountain-climbing film I describe in the chapter on the visceral, exploit this grisly connection. In these films, we and the cameraman are safe; the person he is filming is at risk. If my mountain climber climbs with a safety rope I can appreciate his grace and skill and bravery, but if he is free climbing, completely unprotected, there is no question that I get more of a thrill.

Yet the effect is profoundly unsettling. How much of my thrill comes from waiting for him to die? This isn't Jeff Goldblum under four hours of fly makeup turning into a heap of pus. This is a real man who might die at any moment. Even as I feel the shivers I'm disgusted with myself. I'll get nightmares all right, but they will be triggered by my own sense of guilty fascination. I watch transfixed, but with a sour taste in my mouth.

Reality films like *Mondo Cane*, designed to exploit the raw urges that draw us to the horror film, are calculated to pump us full of visceral kicks without the intermediary of make-believe. The whole appeal of such a film is visceral, and the whole of its visceral appeal is that what is shown isn't make-believe, it's real. Whether it's violence or sex, that is as good a definition as any of pornography.

Porno mates the visceral with the documentary. Simulations are fine for erotica, but porno isn't porno unless it's graphic. The clinical close-up, which I've never heard anyone call erotic, is an icon of the film's reality, a heavy-handed way of proving "See—it's real. We're not faking it."

THE REAL THING

Different as they are, docudrama, documentary, and pornography all claim to be special because they're more "real" than conventional drama. But they aren't more real. All are flashing images on a white wall, bound by the same limitations of the medium: the need to make those flashing images feel three-dimensional; the need to feed audience hunger for story, for sensation, for empathy with the characters; the need to compress and order experience, to have a point of view; the need to leave things out.

These forms aren't any more real than pure drama, but they do have a different relationship with fact. Fact props them up. Fact excuses their shortcomings. The thrill of fact is their claim to fame. If we don't believe them, they are meaningless. If they're not "real," they don't work.

They lean on fact, but they must still address the vicarious, the visceral, and the voyeur in each of us, using techniques which work in any movie. And that is a fine way to convey fact because the filmmaker's techniques are not random experiments but hard-won rules for capturing experience on film. Real, lived experience. In their own fashion, people who make movies are experts on the way human beings perceive their world. And that is as real as it gets.

Some folks far from Hollywood want it to get realer than that. They refuse to seduce the viewer with the illusion of objective reality. Experimental, avant-garde, structuralist, deconstructivist, whatever they call themselves, they eschew Hollywood techniques as tools of propagandistic manipulation. They want to show the viewer he's being used—to make him conscious of the very devices Hollywood labors to conceal.

Michael Snow, for instance, whose film *Wavelength* is a single forty-five-minute zoom from a wide view of a large loft to a close-up of a picture of the ocean tacked on the opposite wall, describes it as an effort "to make a definitive statement of pure Film space and time, a balancing of 'illusion' and 'fact,' all about seeing." He's keeping the viewer at arm's length so the viewer can examine his own responses.

While such films almost dare you to sit through them, they can yield real insight for the patient viewer. From a Hollywood film-maker's perspective they can be particularly illuminating because in pushing technique beyond the point of no return they show just how far one can safely go. When Jean-Luc Godard's *Breathless* came out in 1959, for instance, it seemed as unconventional as *Wavelength* did in the late sixties, yet it was greeted with fascination in Hollywood because it seemed to break the rules and work any-way. Compared to *Wavelength* it was ploddingly conventional—it had real stars, a love story, and a killer-on-the-run plot—but at crucial moments Godard would yank the viewer out of the picture with a series of jump cuts, repeated action, or some other attention-getting device. Yet the pull of his stars, Jean Seberg and Jean-Paul Belmondo, was so strong in the opposite direction that they drew the viewer right back in. While *Breathless* would never appeal to as wide an audience as a Hollywood film requires—Godard is too resolutely abstruse for that—it showed Hollywood filmmakers where they were being timid, and a film like *The Last Detail* could come along and use some of the same techniques in an invisible Hollywood way. Hollywood's arsenal was strengthened by the assault on its domain.

A journalist friend of mine recently got his first job in the movies, as development executive for a film production company. When I asked him how it felt he seemed uneasy. "I saw dailies for the first time the other day," he said. "They were just as boring and repetitious as I expected." "So?" I asked him. "Then last night I saw a movie and I couldn't watch it. It wasn't a continuous experience anymore, it was a bunch of bits strung together." I laughed. He was serious. "I don't think I'll ever be able to really enjoy a movie again."

One week of dailies and my friend had lost his innocence. What happens to the rest of us who work at them? Most of moviemaking is a destructive act. The writing, the rehearsing, the planning, the shooting, the editing are a matter of breaking down the experience: stretching and squeezing each second, parsing the emotions, analyzing each sight and sound. Sound becomes sound effects, story becomes story beats, scenes become shots, relationships become moments. We worry about whether the sound fits the picture, the shots match, the beats are plausible, the moments feel true. Humpty-Dumpty has fallen; how can we ever get him back together again?

Yet in spite of his fears, my friend's disorientation quickly passed. Let philosophers (and avant-garde cineastes) argue over whether there is such a thing as objective reality; we all function as if there were a there out there. Even philosopher David Hume admitted that when he sat down he expected the chair to be beneath him. As moviegoers, we all watch movies as if they were real. We know they aren't, of course. But their persuasive power (which so annoys the experimental filmmaker) is what draws us to the theater. It's a more active process than "suspending disbelief": while we're watching, we want to—even need to—lose ourselves in the world behind the screen.

That creates its own dangers. If we believe in movie worlds too completely, we come to judge our own experience by movie standards. Are our friends as witty, our jobs as exciting, our loves as grand? How much unhappiness have these fantasy expectations caused?

Worse, if we're not careful we come to expect our lives to make the same sort of sense movies make. People want things to add up; that's one reason they find fiction in any medium so satisfying. But things don't. Not in this life. The unfairness of the world is a cruel fact we all contend with. Is our nagging sense of life's randomness and injustice soothed by escape into the better world movies provide? Isn't it truer to say that our unhappiness with our lot is triggered by comparison with the vivid and misleading completeness of the film experience? The avant-gardists have a point.

The problem takes on a whole different dimension for those who make the films. Hume, much as he thought and wrote about the subjectivity of perception, didn't have to spend his days breaking events into bits of image and sound, polishing the bits, and putting them back together again. What does that do to the filmmaker's sense of the there out there?

If loss of innocence is the price of knowledge, understanding is its reward. Philosophers may theorize about subjectivity, but working filmmakers try to learn exactly what it means to say that time is flexible, a function of our inner clock. They study how long a second really is, and how short, and what makes it feel one way or the other. They know that what we see isn't really what's out there because they've learned how spatial perception varies with angle and focal length and lighting, how "true" colors are a figment of lighting, and context, and even the glass of the lens. They know there is no "real" sound but only a better or worse approximation of what our ear expects. Moreover, they precisely explore how all these things shift their meaning depending on what experience they are looking for, the voyeuristic, the vicarious, or the visceral. The philosopher may say absolute reality doesn't exist; the Hollywood filmmaker pretends to understand exactly how it doesn't. That is heady stuff.

But that is only the half of it. Psychologists may theorize about what makes people tick; filmmakers must make them tick. Characters act; and, like it or not, what they do must make sense. Film-makers study emotional nuance, attune themselves to emotional truth. In the presence of great performances they must acknowledge that emotional truth doesn't depend on a real situation sparking appropriate feelings, that great acting mimics genuine emotion to such perfection as to be indistinguishable from the real thing, except that it is more true, more intense and credible, than documentary reality. If filmmakers aren't careful, it becomes the standard by which they judge emotion in life—and as in film, they may even expect it to happen on command.

The danger isn't in the knowledge but in its use. The purpose of all this understanding is control. Filmmakers use their knowledge of how we see and hear what we think is out there to goad us into feeling what they want us to feel, to make a moment funny or tragic or disgusting or pathetic or uplifting or simply matter of fact. The filmmaker can make us part of the event or a dispassionate observer; can make us admire a character or despise him. The filmmaker can even make us feel we understand him. Shaping experience is the supreme pleasure of manipulating film.

Such autocratic power makes for difficult people. If filmmakers think they can manipulate the real world the way they manipulate film, if they forget that real relationships are reciprocal, not like one-way transactions with the screen, they will be bitterly disappointed. When life gets messy, when friends or family mutiny, it's all too easy to retreat into the malleable world of film, and then even the films suffer. If movies replace life as the norm, the film-maker's work comes to reflect not life's conflicts but film's certainties, and it ossifies.

But that doesn't have to happen. Sven Nykvist, the legendary Swedish cinematographer, once said to me that the picture he was working on was his hundred and fourth film. I could see he was as worried as any neophyte about getting the job done right. I asked him how he managed to maintain his enthusiasm. "You seem to think of it as your first film," I remarked.

"The secret is not that I think of it as my first film," he replied, "but that I think of it as my last."

Nykvist spoke the truth. The filmmaker's greatest fear isn't that his work will be taken out of his control, or butchered, or reviled. His worst fear is that he will never be able to make another film.

6

HOLLYWOOD

VERSUS THE WORLD

I've been talking about Hollywood filmmaking as if it were the natural outcome of the way the human animal sees, and hears, and thinks. It is based, after all, on the fundamental supposition that what works for me will work for you, whoever you are. But will it? If film technique is so fundamentally rooted, what makes Hollywood films feel so different from other films around the world?

I believe the basic principles I've described, the ABCs of film perception, are equally valid in Beijing, Budapest, or Bombay. While I can say with certainty that a Godard film like *Weekend* would never be made in Hollywood, the way Godard plays with the medium is based on assumptions about film that he learned watching Ford and Hitchcock. What Godard chooses to do with his knowledge is what makes his movies different.

"Hollywood," of course, is an amorphous term. Hollywood has always been a haven for the emigré, from Erich von Stroheim to Miloš Forman, but since the breakup of the studio system one doesn't even have to be a first-generation American to make Hollywood movies. A Hollywood film can be shot in London or Rome or Morocco or Yugoslavia by a Dutch director like Paul Verhoeven, with an Australian star like Mel Gibson, a British writer like Robert Bolt, a Swedish cameraman like Sven Nykvist, an Italian art director like Ferdinando Scarfiotti, and an Israeli producer like Mena-

OPPOSITE PAGE
TOP: *Rambo: First Blood Part II*, BOTTOM: *The Battle of Algiers*

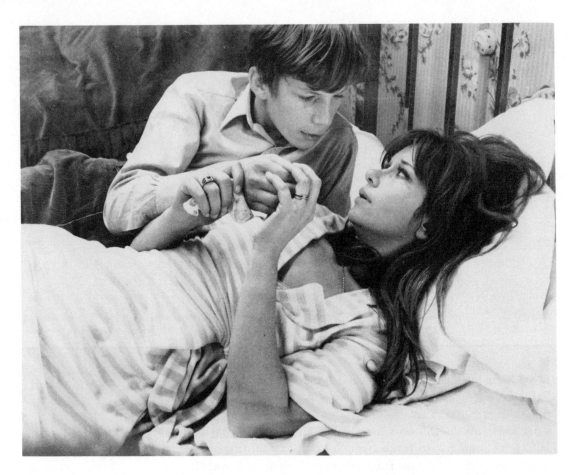

Murmur of the Heart

OPPOSITE PAGE
Rebel Without a Cause

chem Golan. It can be financed by a Japanese consortium, scored by the London Philharmonic, and edited by a Frenchwoman in the Hamptons. But the films I'm talking about all share one thing in common: all "Hollywood" films are made for mass distribution in the United States, which means they are made with an eye for what some large segment of the American public wants to see. Hollywood is in the eye of the beholder.

Hollywood is oceanic in its diversity, yet a "Hollywood style" is as hard to deny as it is to define. It is easy to set up amusing comparisons—*Animal House* versus *La Dolce Vita*, *Rambo* versus *The Battle of Algiers*, *Annie Hall* versus *Claire's Knee*, *Rebel Without a Cause* versus *Murmur of the Heart*, *The Godfather* versus *Pelle the Conqueror*, *Cocoon* versus *Tokyo Story*, *Star Wars* versus *Solaris*, *Sixteen Candles* versus *The Virgin Spring*, the Bond films versus the Apu Trilogy. Hollywood films have more bang, more flash, more sizzle, more pace, more plot, more everything but depth of

character and insight into the human condition. You might say, as did André Malraux, that Americans spend a great deal of effort denying that life is essentially tragic. But what about *The Godfather* or *One Flew Over the Cuckoo's Nest?* You might say that Hollywood films are skewed more toward the visceral and the voyeuristic than their foreign counterparts. But what about Chinese kung fu films (what *Variety* calls the "chop-sockeys") or the lavish, plotty, ridiculous Bombay musical dramas? What makes a Hollywood film unique?

The best way to dig down to essentials is not to compare disparate films but to find two films, one from inside and one from outside Hollywood, that are as close as possible—and then scrutinize their differences. Not fringe or gray-area films that blur the distinction between us and them, like Woody Allen's *Interiors* or one of Akira

Citizen Kane

Kurosawa's Samurai Westerns, but strong examples of their respective film traditions. Consider *Citizen Kane* and *8½*.

Citizen Kane is an acknowledged Hollywood masterpiece; *8½* is often cited as the quintessential arty European film which could never possibly be made in Hollywood. Yet these films are much more similar than you might realize. While both films are highly stylized, in both style is trying to be invisible—it is there to deepen the experience, not make the audience self-consciously aware of the limits of film, as Godard might. Technique serves to mirror reality. As Federico Fellini has his alter ego say in *8½*, "I want to put a character up on the screen, without lies." Except for Fellini's dream and fantasy sequences, his dialogue, performance, character motivation and behavior are as resolutely naturalistic as Orson Welles.' And in their own way Fellini's dreams and fantasies are

8½

naturalistic too: the fantasies are there to show us what really goes on in the character's head, and the dream sequences come as close as any, ever, to capturing the actual dream experience on film.

Both films have tightly packed, fast-paced, fluidly staged scenes (if anything, Fellini's scenes have more going on in them than Welles'), constructed in the conventional way with beginnings, middles, and ends and edited for spatial and temporal continuity. Both have humorous counterpoint. Fellini is just as concerned as Welles with entertaining his audience—his film has a visceral, erotic edge missing from *Kane*, and he matches Welles' love of cinematic magic with his circus entertainer's desire to cram his film with everything that amuses, as his alter ego, Guido, remarks when he auditions a passing tap dancer.

Both films share the same fundamental story concern: they are character studies held together by the magnetism of a star at their center. Both portray powerful, unsatisfied men, men justly accused of manipulating those around them in order to be loved when they themselves are incapable of loving. We even see both men's marriages destroyed by their dalliances with shallow but affectionate mistresses.

Thematically, both concern the efforts of a celebrated character to come to terms with himself. While 8½ is avowedly autobiographical—with Marcello Mastroianni standing in for the director—in *Citizen Kane* the director himself plays the lead, and in hindsight his character cuts chillingly close to the bone. *Kane* ends tragically, on a downbeat, more "European" note, while 8½ actually pulls off what Hollywood would appreciatively call a "life-affirming" ending. Yet *Citizen Kane* is quintessentially Hollywood and 8½ is inconceivable here. What's the difference?

Simply put, compared to watching *Kane*, watching 8½ feels like work. Rewarding, but hard.

8½ is more of a personal rumination, *Citizen Kane* is more of a story. Now this is a matter of degree. Fellini is a showman, but he is first and foremost concerned with getting it right. He wants to show all the complexity of life, all the conflicts, ambivalences, and ambiguities of his character, without lies, and he'll use anything that will get him closer to the truth—a dream, a fantasy, a random happenstance. He's assuming that if he gets it right we'll get it too, if we're smart and hip enough.

Welles' first priority is to grab and hold his audience. He wants to get his character right as well, but he overlays that concern with

a desire to carry us along, to make sure we get the movie the first time we see it, even if we're not particularly smart or hip. I walk out of *8½* and I feel I've been a privileged witness to the mysteries of the human soul, but I don't feel I've *understood* it in the simple-minded way I got *Citizen Kane*. When I see the films a second time, I realize the mysteries of *Kane* and the underlying simplicity of *8½*. But *Kane* wants to be sure I feel like I got it the first time.

In practical terms, this means there is more plot in *Citizen Kane* and things are more spelled out. The story thread that runs through *8½* is whether Mastroianni as Guido will make his next film. Guido keeps stalling and putting everyone off, but finally the decision forces him face-to-face with what he really wants from life. Finally, he stops fighting his ambivalence and bails out of making the movie, and he feels freed up, liberated by his acceptance of his own conflicts and eccentricities. We are, too.

Guido creates worlds of his own as a filmmaker; Charles Foster Kane tries to remake the world in his own image. He succeeds more than any man has a right to. But because he never reaches the kind

The finale to *8½*

of self-acceptance Guido finds in 8½, his is a hollow victory. Kane is a man who desperately needs to be loved but won't admit it, a man incapable of love himself and blind to his failing. Kane's manipulations and intransigence finally isolate him from those who try to love him, and leave him pitifully alone.

But *Citizen Kane* the movie isn't only the story of a man fighting life. It's a detective story too, the reporter's search for the meaning of Kane's last words. Instead of Fellini's question, "Will Guido shoot his film?" Welles asks, "What is Rosebud?"

The difference is crucial. Welles' is a simpler, more straightforward question. In 8½ I share Guido's own confusion, which is Fellini's point. How do I know whether I want Guido to shoot his film? How do I know whether it is a good script or will be good for him? But I sure as hell want to know what Rosebud is, and at the end of *Kane* I sure find out, even if I don't quite get what Kane's life was all about.

The search for Rosebud lets the filmmakers guide the viewer through the thicket of experience. It lets them open their film with a bald statement of what Kane has done, and it lets someone ask right out, "Who is Kane the man?" It lets us have ongoing commentary from the people in the present that points us at what the scenes of Kane's life are about. It gives a sense of closure to the story of a frustrated life, the very kind of closure Fellini works to avoid.

Welles is telling us a great story. Fellini is telling us *his* story. All films are collaborative, but Fellini's film is as close to an auteur work as a man who only directs the movie can get. We feel the vision is his, no matter how many writers were on the project (perhaps because there were so many writers). The elliptical flow of the film, the play between the present and the director's memories and fantasies, feels intensely personal. Who but Fellini could have conceived his dream sequences?

Welles, however, was the captain of a ship. Rosebud is a clever plot device. It solves a tough story problem brilliantly. There's no reason why Welles should have had to be the one to think it up. In fact, the film is a masterpiece of artful construction, a monumental achievement by its writer, Herman Mankiewicz.

8½ is beautifully photographed, but the stylistic signature of the film doesn't depend on the particular genius of the camerman. With a different cinematographer 8½ would have been substantially the same film. *Citizen Kane*, however, owes its famous look to Gregg Toland's innovative experiments in low-angle deep-focus

Toland's deep focus photography in *Citizen Kane*

photography. *Kane* wouldn't have been *Kane* without him. Welles was a great director and a renowned egomaniac, but *Citizen Kane* is a great film because Welles the producer assembled an extraordinary group of filmmakers and Welles the director knew how to get the most out of them.

Can you imagine a director outside of Hollywood, a French or a Japanese or a German director, saying John Ford's proud line; "It's just a job of work, that's all . . . you do the best you can . . . like the man digging the ditch who says 'I hope the ground is soft so that my pick digs deeper'?" Can you imagine a Latin American or a Russian or a Swedish director using the words of Billy Wilder, "If I don't bore people and I keep my crew working then I am a success"? False modesty aside, these men are describing a distinct attitude toward their work and its product—work based on an American idea of team play, which is possible because the end result is first and foremost not a personal statement but something made to grab and hold an audience.

I didn't realize how odd the Hollywood attitude was until I went to Pune, not far from Bombay, for a couple of months to teach Hollywood-style filmmaking at the Film and Television Institute of India. I must admit I went with a certain amount of first-world arrogance. India makes more films than we do, but its cinema is better known for its quantity than its quality. I thought I could share some good old American know-how with the Indian students. I assumed they would be eager to learn how it's done by people who, by their standards, have all the film, equipment, and time in the world.

They gasped with incredulity when I told them the favorite Hollywood phrase "film is cheap" (meaning "if in doubt, shoot it"). They were shocked, some were even offended, at the thought of a director letting the camerman choose the camera setup. They were skeptical at the idea of covering a scene from more than one angle and quoted Robert Bresson that there is only one right shot for any moment. But the first thing I learned was that Hollywood looks very small from over there. I was viewed with affectionate curiosity as an emissary of an aberrant offshoot of world cinema that specializes in slick but empty productions of a mild, superficial appeal. I could see their point, particularly since their diet of recent American films consisted of *Rambo* and the *Police Academy* series. But they all liked Hitchcock, so I thought I'd start there and win them over.

My Indian students liked Hitchcock, all right, but they weren't especially interested in learning from him. The subtleties of his craft which so fascinated me just didn't seem to matter to them, not because they couldn't see them but because they weren't interest in doing what he did.

I discovered that instead of telling them how we do it in Hollywood I had to convince them what we did was worth doing at all. The students were as bright, well informed, and passionate about film as any American students, but they didn't seem to care whether their stories were credible, or their characters motivated, or their films tightly constructed. "People believe whatever you put on the screen," I was told. The basic assumptions I'd always taken for granted just weren't there.

You can't teach a basic assumption. How can you make someone care if a story is credible? A few weeks of facing this polite indifference and I felt as if I were fighting for my life. If my basic beliefs were built on quicksand, what had I been doing for the last twenty years?

I should have realized what I was in for the first day, when I met the Professor of Film Appreciation. He was tall, elegant, and spoke impeccable Oxbridge British. He happened to mention that he was a filmmaker as well as a teacher and was currently working on a script. "Oh," I asked naively, "what kind of story is it?" He made a languid deprecatory gesture. My question was beside the point. "Many of our filmmakers, and I count myself among them, have a more highly developed sensibility than their audience."

Not invisibility but impenetrability was what this man was after. He was eager to push the bounds of cinema, to explore new concepts of time and space, and he wouldn't mind at all if he was so far ahead of people that they couldn't follow him. It might even convince him he was right.

I learned that the first exercise the Professor of Screenwriting assigned his first-year students was to write a scene of a man alone in a room for six hours, no telephones or fantasy sequences allowed. The plan was to give the students a sense of how film can handle time and space using only "sights and sounds," unencumbered by conflict or story. For a Hollywood screenwriter, this would be like walking unencumbered by gravity. When I left, the second-year students were raptly attending lectures by a prominent Indian filmmaker on "the Bergsonian concept of time."

Certainly there is nothing wrong with this sort of filmmaking. It's filmmakers' filmmaking, and it is important to the art form to have people out there on the edge. But should it be the primary goal of the only real film school in India, a country making six-hundred-odd movies a year for an audience of hundreds of millions? Why is so much effort devoted to making movies almost no one can understand?

The students admitted to me that by the end of their three years they were making films they wouldn't have sat through when they entered the school. I accused them of abdicating their responsibility to their friends and family. They taught me the realities of Indian filmmaking. The industry is polarized, they explained, between government-sponsored experimental cinema and commercial movies, the Bombay film, a formulaic exercise in kitsch. A few filmmakers fight the system, struggling to make their own films for a larger audience and then shoehorn them into theaters. But it's an uphill battle. The system—the producers, the distributors, the theater owners, the government funding mechanisms—conspires against them.

Bombay films are fun, if you like pizzas with the works, but only an ignoramus would make a diet of them. They are truly product in that they're made not for the filmmaker but for the audience. Actors work on fifty at a time. Scripts appear in bits the day of shooting. Crews are put together for a few days' work and then dismantled. The filmmakers (some Institute graduates) justify their films by their success, but judging from the interviews I've read, they don't show any particular pride in what they've made. It's not expected of them. They know what a good movie is, they're saying, they're just not allowed to make one because their audiences wouldn't want to see it.

The Indian faculty and students shared the same assumption. And I'm not sure it can be blamed entirely on the system. The conviction ran deeper than that. Deep down, they didn't believe they could make a movie they were proud of that masses of people would want to see. *Their* movie had to tap the part of themselves which made them more discriminating than the common herd.

What makes Hollywood films different, I maintain, is that the industry runs on the opposite assumption. In their simple-minded, greedy, democratic way Hollywood filmmakers know deep in their gut that they can have it both ways—they can make a film they are terrifically proud of that masses of people will want to see, too. That means tuning out their more rarefied sensibilities and using that part of themselves they share with their parents and their siblings, with Wall Street lawyers and small-town Rotarians and waiters and engineering students, with cops and pacifists and the guys at the car wash and perhaps even second graders and junkies and bigots; that part that Hitchcock or Chaplin touch so effortlessly, the common human currency of joy and sorrow and anger and excitement and loss and pain and love.

Hollywood films may be botched or incompetent, cynical or crass, but they are usually the best the filmmakers can do. Hollywood filmmakers have made a pact with their mass audience: for reasons of greed, ego, and simple curiosity they try to give everyone what they'd like to see themselves.

OVERLEAF
The Gold Rush

INDEX

Note: page numbers in *italics* refer to illustrations

PHOTO CREDITS

The author gratefully acknowledges the assistance of: the Academy of Motion Picture Arts and Sciences; Terry Geeskin and the Museum of Modern Art Film Stills Department; Mark Wanamaker and the Bison Archives; John Neuhart; Zipporah Films; Maysles Films Inc.; Errol Morris; Warner Bros. Publicity Department; Twentieth Century Fox Film Corporation Publicity Department; Lucasfilm Ltd., Clinica Estetico, Ltd.; and MacGillivray Freeman Films.

ABOUT THE AUTHOR

JON BOORSTIN grew up in Chicago, studied at Harvard University, and trained as an architect at Trinity College, Cambridge. He worked designing exhibits and making films for the Office of Charles and Ray Eames before leaving to make his own award-winning documentaries, including *Exploratorium*, which was nominated for an Academy Award for Best Documentary Short. He became involved in feature films as American Film Institute intern on the Warren Beatty thriller *The Parallax View*, and continued to work with its director, Alan Pakula, as associate producer of *All the President's Men*. Jon Boorstin's first script as a writer, *Dream Lover*, was produced by Mr. Boorstin for MGM. It won the Grand Prix at the Festival International du Film Fantastique in Avoriaz, France. He has since written for films and television (and *To the Limit* for IMAX, the world's largest film format) and is an occasional columnist for the Los Angeles *Times*, for which he writes "Letters to My Mother-in-Law" about family life with his wife, Leni, their eight-year-old son, Eric, and their five-year-old daughter, Ariel.